"As Christians we all strongly affirm servant leadersh. [...] Elmer leads us on a pilgrimage on what this means in ([...] another book of quick and easy formulas to be appliec [...] ...s. It is a call to a new way of relating to one another and to those [...] ...u us. It is not only for Christian ministers and missionaries, but for all of us as parents, teachers and colleagues. The danger is that if we read this carefully and embody its deep insights, it might make servanthood a part of our lives as Christians in this world."

PAUL G. HIEBERT, DISTINGUISHED PROFESSOR OF MISSION AND ANTHROPOLOGY, TRINITY EVANGELICAL DIVINITY SCHOOL, AND AUTHOR OF *INCARNATIONAL MINISTRY*

"Dr. Duane Elmer is my good friend and mentor, and I have learned a lot from him: not only from his teachings and writings but also from our relationship. He lives every day what he believes. I highly recommend his book *Cross-Cultural Servanthood: Serving the World in Christlike Humility*. This book, in my opinion, is going to be God's instrument for blessing many people and a great help for people from every nation, every language and in every position. May God bless the book and its author!"

NIKOLAY NEDELCHEV, PRESIDENT, EUROPEAN EVANGELICAL ALLIANCE, AND EXECUTIVE DIRECTOR, BULGARIAN EVANGELICAL THEOLOGICAL INSTITUTE

"Elmer's wisdom in preparing people for cross-cultural service comes across clearly throughout this wonderful book. His humbly told stories interwoven with carefully explained truths invited me to revisit things I wish I had done differently in my cross-cultural work and to reflect on the areas in which God still has work to do in my life. Simply put, this marvelous book opens significant doors to more effective cross-cultural service. If all missionaries lived out the lessons Elmer presents, the effect on missionary service and outreach—not to mention the church— would be incalculable."

SCOTT MOREAU, DEPARTMENT CHAIR AND PROFESSOR OF INTERCULTURAL STUDIES, WHEATON COLLEGE, AND COAUTHOR OF *INTRODUCING WORLD MISSIONS*

"With effective illustrations and ready-to-implement practical applications, Duane Elmer reminds us that Jesus-style servanthood must be biblically understood and culturally applied—in ways that the recipients interpret as servanthood. This book should be required reading for every Christian seeking to serve cross-culturally, whether in a long-term or short-term capacity."

PAUL BORTHWICK, AUTHOR OF *HOW TO BE A WORLD-CLASS CHRISTIAN* AND *A MIND FOR MISSIONS*

"The relationship between task effectiveness and relational effectiveness is a crucial issue for missionaries and Christian workers of all kinds. Duane Elmer has pinpointed the essential linchpin—servanthood. He ably shows how Jesus' example of servanthood enables one to honor others while honoring God."

MICHELE RICKETT, FOUNDER AND PRESIDENT, SISTERS IN SERVICE, AND COAUTHOR OF *DAUGHTERS OF HOPE*

"*Cross-Cultural Servanthood* is needed more today than ever in the history of missions. In today's mission context, millions of short-term missionaries travel cross-culturally every year. Tens of thousands of non-Western missionaries serve in almost every country of the world. Many churches from the West are forming partnerships with churches from other countries. In all these scenarios, there is a tendency toward an attitude of superiority. The danger of ethnocentric arrogance is exploding. Dr. Elmer provides crucial principles of servanthood illustrated with timely examples. Short- and long-term missionaries from the West as well as the non-Western world need to read and practice the principles of this book. God's glory in the nations is at stake!"

JAMES E. PLUEDDEMANN, FORMER INTERNATIONAL DIRECTOR OF SIM, AND PROFESSOR OF INTERCULTURAL STUDIES, TRINITY EVANGELICAL DIVINITY SCHOOL

"My library is filled with books, tapes and materials all on servanthood in which I see and hear the oft-repeated phrase 'servant-leader.' But how do we live as servants or 'slaves' in a cross-cultural context? Duane Elmer has provided a much-needed cultural guide for any of us involved in intercultural ministry. His writing gives us a biblical foundation along with living anecdotes from across the world in real-life situations. Duane helps us understand the lifelong process and guides us through the matrix of personality, cultural and generational differences. I believe his comments on the mantra 'servant-leader' were especially needed."

JOHN H. ORME, EXECUTIVE DIRECTOR, IFMA

"As the Son of God entered first-century Jewish culture and discerned and used its expressions of servanthood—a basin and a towel—to communicate the nature of his heavenly Father, Duane Elmer draws helpfully from Scripture and his broad experience to help us enter another culture today and discern and use its expressions of servanthood to communicate the nature of our heavenly Father as well."

J. DUDLEY WOODBERRY, DEAN EMERITUS AND PROFESSOR OF ISLAMIC STUDIES, SCHOOL OF INTERCULTURAL STUDIES, FULLER THEOLOGICAL SEMINARY

"Elmer provides a fresh and provocative look at learning and ministering cross-culturally through the scriptural mandate to be servants of the master engaged in kingdom work. Noting that the practice of servanthood must vary in every culture, the book provides powerful and practical insights into how to become an effective servant in another culture. This is an excellent resource for practical mission training, and for those already in ministry, the book enables willing servants to sharpen their emotional and behavioral practices to more appropriate contextualized servanthood."

SHERWOOD LINGENFELTER, PROVOST, SENIOR VICE PRESIDENT AND PROFESSOR OF ANTHROPOLOGY, FULLER THEOLOGICAL SEMINARY, AND COAUTHOR OF *MINISTERING CROSS-CULTURALLY*

CROSS-CULTURAL SERVANTHOOD

Serving the World in Christlike Humility

DUANE ELMER

IVP Books

An imprint of InterVarsity Press
Downers Grove, Illinois

InterVarsity Press
P.O. Box 1400, Downers Grove, IL 60515-1426
World Wide Web: www.ivpress.com
E-mail: email@ivpress.com

©2006 by Duane H. Elmer

All rights reserved. No part of this book may be reproduced in any form without written permission from InterVarsity Press.

InterVarsity Press® is the book-publishing division of InterVarsity Christian Fellowship/USA®, a student movement active on campus at hundreds of universities, colleges and schools of nursing in the United States of America, and a member movement of the International Fellowship of Evangelical Students. For information about local and regional activities, write Public Relations Dept., InterVarsity Christian Fellowship/USA, 6400 Schroeder Rd., P.O. Box 7895, Madison, WI 53707-7895, or visit the IVCF website at <www.intervarsity.org>.

All Scripture quotations, unless otherwise indicated, are taken from the Holy Bible, New International Version®. NIV®. Copyright ©1973, 1978, 1984 by International Bible Society. Used by permission of Zondervan Publishing House. All rights reserved.

Design: Cindy Kiple

Images: globe: Digital Vision/Getty Images
puzzle piece: Pierre-Yves Goavec

ISBN 978-0-8308-3378-8

Printed in the United States of America ∞

 InterVarsity Press is committed to protecting the environment and to the responsible use of natural resources. As a member of the Green Press Initiative we use recycled paper whenever possible. To learn more about the Green Press Initiative, visit <www.greenpressinitiative.org>.

Library of Congress Cataloging-in-Publication Data

Elmer, Duane, 1943-
Cross-cultural servanthood: serving the world in christlike
humility / by Duane H. Elmer.
  p. cm.
Includes bibliographical references.
ISBN-13: 978-0-8308-3378-8 (pbk.: alk. paper)
ISBN-10: 0-8308-3378-1 (pbk.: alk. paper)
1. Service (Theology) 2. Jesus Christ—Servanthood. 3.
Intercultural communication—Religious aspects—Christianity. I.
Title.
BT738.4.E46 2006
266'.023—dc22

                                                                    2005033143

P   24   23   22   21   20   19   18   17   16

Y   23   22   21   20   19   18   17   16

To Five
Who served me and their world
Each differently, distinctively, wonderfully
Bob, Chuck, Dave, Don, Wayne
Thank You

And to my wife, Muriel, my beloved,
Awesome in her servanthood to all

Contents

Part One

SERVANTHOOD
Basic Perspectives

1

SERVANTHOOD
Its Burden and Challenge

*"I don't know what your destiny will be, but one thing I know:
the only ones among you who will be really happy
are those who have sought and found how to serve."*

ALBERT SCHWEITZER

*"We are not called to help people.
We are called to follow Jesus, in whose service we learn
who we are and how we are to help and be helped."*

STANLEY HAUERWAS AND WILLIAM H. WILLIMON

"So what would you like for breakfast tomorrow morning?" inquired my wife. The answer slipped easily from my mouth: "Eggs, bacon and toast." We were on our honeymoon, and this would be the first meal she would cook in our married life. The next morning I heard the pots and pans, and soon the aroma, the right aroma, drifted past my nostrils. The words "It's ready" brought me to the kitchen, where she was seated at the small table, candle burning in the center and expectation in her eyes.

I sat down and said, "Let's give thanks," but before I closed my eyes to pray I caught a glimpse of what was on my plate. Startled I said, "Oh, what's this?" to which she answered, "That's your eggs, bacon and toast. Why?" Concern had replaced the look of expectation. Innocently, I responded, "What did you do to the eggs?" "I poached them. Why do you ask?" she queried. It was my turn to answer in this exchange of questions that wasn't going to take us anywhere good. "Why would anybody do such an immoral thing to an egg?" I said with some seriousness and some playfulness. It was too late to be playful. I was hoping for a discussion on the art of cooking eggs, but she had already left the room in tears.

Sooner or later it was bound to happen. My wife, born and raised in Zimbabwe with a Canadian mother, brought a strong British influence to our marriage. I, being raised in rural southern Wisconsin in a Swiss community, grew up on fried eggs cooked over medium, lots of bacon and crispy toast. Occasionally my mother would scramble the eggs just to stretch our "horizons," but we knew that tomorrow morning she would be back in the groove. I had never seen a poached egg, and when it lay there on my plate, barely cooked (I should say barely warm!), tactfulness got lost in the confusion surrounding a simple difference in the way we enjoyed eggs.

My wife's desire to serve me in this simple but meaningful event was misinterpreted and badly handled by me. *I was not thinking servanthood.* I didn't understand her cultural history, and she didn't understand mine. Both of us felt rejected. What should have been a beautiful moment turned sour.

This story marks both the simplicity and complexity of cross-cultural servanthood. Servanthood is revealed in simple, everyday events. But it's complex because servanthood is culturally defined—that is, serving must be sensitive to the cultural landscape while remaining true to the Scripture. That is both the challenge and burden of servanthood—and of this book.

The following pages will unpack the idea of cross-cultural servanthood. While not being easy, it is the calling of every person who wishes to follow Jesus, whether in your home culture or beyond. The principles in this book apply to a wide range of Christians—in one sense, to all who want to serve others. Illustrations from marriage, inner-city ministry, community development programs, church planting efforts, Bible schools and seminaries, relief and development activities, and reconciliation efforts will reveal the relevance of these principles in a wide variety of situations. Because these thoughts are drawn from the Scripture, from cross-cultural research and the experiences of people from numerous countries, the intended audience is not only Westerners but those who wish to serve God and his people regardless of their home country. Whether you are going short term or long term, engaging in relief and development or church planting, teaching in a Bible school or working in medicine, whether the ministry is rural or urban, this book should help you achieve your first priority: to serve God and those around you.

THE SON OF GOD ENTERED HUMAN CULTURE

The ways we are effective in culture are also the primary ways we serve others. We serve people by entering into a *relationship* of love and mutual commitment. As the apostle Paul says, "We loved you so much that we were delighted to share with you not only the gospel of God but our lives as well" (1 Thess 2:8). In the early stages servanthood may be best seen when we are willing to *adjust* to the local cultural patterns, including learning the language. Jesus came into our human context (Jn 1:14), adjusted to the Jewish culture (Lk 2:52) and lived among us so that when the time was right he would accomplish the redemption of all who would believe. This, of course, is *task* effectiveness. Jesus served us exquisitely in each of these three areas, suggesting that in the same way we can be a servant to others.

This book is about servanthood, focusing primarily on *relationship* factors and the *adjustment* factors. I believe that most people going overseas are quite well equipped in *task* effectiveness; that is, they are technically competent to do the job because most schools and workshops focus on job skills. This book focuses on relational and adjustment competency so that the servant spirit we wish to portray will, in fact, be seen and valued by the local people. All three competencies must be present in the servant for any of one them to be successful.

A MOST UNNATURAL TASK

I must confess that anyone writing a book on servanthood must be a little audacious—maybe more than a little. It's really quite an unnatural task. Writers should not only know their topic but also live consistently with it. Few Christians I know would claim to know about being a servant much less say they live a servant life in a cross-cultural situation. Most of us in international or interethnic ministry, however, do have it as an aspiration. This book is for those, including myself, who aspire to be cross-cultural servants.

Furthermore, I have no pretense about superior knowledge of the topic and I certainly lay no claim to modeling servanthood better than anyone else. In fact, I probably struggle more than most. In reality, I think I am below average on the matter.

Finally, it isn't really my choice to write this book. For fifteen years I have been reading and researching the topic, gathering stacks of articles and ideas and interviewing people in numerous countries. Many people, having heard me on this topic, have asked if the material is in print, and it wasn't, until now. Nevertheless, I have procrastinated in every way possible, hoping to avoid this moment. Yet here I am writing and still resisting, certainly feeling inadequate. But I am convinced God has birthed this work—at least I pray so.

I have been around missionaries much of my adult life. In fact I was a missionary for a good chunk of my life. The repeated ambition among missionaries is to be a "servant." "I want to serve God, serve the people, serve the church" is the frequent theme heard within this community of people, and it certainly is a worthy and biblical goal.

While I was hearing future missionaries describe their desire to be servants, I was also traveling widely in other countries. As I made initial friendships and renewed old ones with various international people, I asked many of them one question: What could missionaries do to more effectively minister the gospel of Christ in your culture? I was not sure what I was expecting. But the answers did surprise me. Many said that they valued the missionary presence and the love they felt from them. But many said, with hesitation but conviction, "Missionaries could more effectively minister the gospel of Christ if they did not think they were so superior to us." Several said virtually those exact words, and others made statements approximating it. I was stunned. I assumed, at first, that I was just talking to a few discontented people. But over time I realized their motives were pure and their comments were made out of deep concern for the integrity of the gospel in their country.

MY OWN CONFESSION

Upon returning to South Africa and talking with former students of mine, I learned from them that I too fell into the category of acting superior. I didn't know it at the time and would have been mortified to have thought it true, but it was. Plain and simple, it was true of me, and I am ashamed.

The need for teachers was critical, and there was no time for culture learning. Since instruction was in English I could plunge in. But I could only teach from my cultural context, so my illustrations, emphases and applications were all more fitting to a North American church culture. The issues among the believers in South Africa were very different. Furthermore, I am not sure my ability to learn about their culture was very well developed. Consequently, I easily fell into the heavy lecture mode and went home at the end of the day feeling good that I had "taught" them. A devastating assumption was buried deep within me: I had been trained and I knew what was good for these students. That raw arrogance spilled over into other parts of my missionary life and, while evident to my students and other local people, did not emerge into my own awareness until years later. That awareness led me on a journey.

Having found myself among the guilty, I resolved to understand several things. First, why are some people, who say they intend to serve, perceived as having attitudes of superiority, paternalism or neocolonialism— all opposites of servanthood. Serving while holding an attitude of superiority (even unconsciously) is like, as someone has said, "trying to push a bus while sitting inside of it." It's not going to happen!

Second, I wanted to find out how the people in other countries perceive servanthood. What does that mean for anyone who wishes to serve Christ and the people of other cultures? Third, I wanted to find out how the Scripture defined *servant*. In the Old Testament the nation Israel is frequently called a "servant," and so is the Messiah as well as Moses and other leaders. In the New Testament Christ came as humble, obedient servant (Phil 2). Servanthood is a powerful theme in Scripture and the character and function of a servant are quite well defined.

Fourth, I wanted to find out what the social sciences have discovered about the effective cross-cultural worker. Social science researchers do not use the words *serve* or *servant* very often but are deeply committed to effectiveness and adaptation. Last, I wanted to know if there was some agreement between what host-country people, the Scripture and the social science literature said. If there were congruities, what would the servant person look like?

PRELIMINARY THOUGHTS

Many missionaries may be like me: well intentioned, dedicated and wanting to serve, but also naive and in some denial about what it means to serve in *another culture*. The reality is that many of us want to serve from our own cultural context. That is, we believe that servanthood everywhere else probably looks like it does in our own culture. In fact, I am inclined to think that there's a little switch in our head somewhere. When we call ourselves a servant, the switch is triggered and we automatically believe that everything we do from there on will epitomize servanthood. In other words, calling ourselves a servant means we are a servant. If others cannot see it, that is their problem.

Many missionaries may be like me in another way: I *am* often guilty of a superior attitude. Submerged deep within me, it is evasive and hard to identify. I quickly rationalize and deny its presence. Usually superiority appears in disguises that pretend to be virtues—virtues such as

- I need to correct their error (meaning I have superior knowledge, a corner on truth).

- My education has equipped me to know what is best for you (so let me do most of the talking while you do most of the listening and changing).

- I am here to help you (so do as I say).

- I can be your spiritual mentor (so I am your role model).

- Let me disciple you, equip you, train you (often perceived as "let me make you into a clone of myself").

These and other so-called virtues corrupt our attempts to serve others. I think my students saw these "virtues" in me. Superiority cloaked in the desire to serve is still superiority. It's not our words that count but the perceptions of the local people who watch our lives and sense our attitudes.

Added to this hidden and evasive superiority is the dilemma of living in a North American culture that often tells us we are the most powerful, the most technically advanced, the richest, the best educated, the leader of the free world, the . . . Even though these are at best partially true, the message of superiority seeps into the brain, revealing itself in subtle but offensive ways. Because it's unthinkable for most of us to name these subtle expressions as superiorities, we spin them as virtues. Yet others may see them for what they are: an attitude of superiority. The Bible calls it pride. I speak primarily to people, like myself, who were socialized mostly in mainstream, white American culture and assimilated the cultural values, often uncritically. I leave it to people of other ethnicities and nationalities to judge these matters for themselves.

CULTURAL MISINTERPRETATION

I don't believe, however, that the problem can be attributed only to a superior attitude. I know too many missionaries who don't have an attitude problem. Even so, they may still find themselves charged with exuding superiority—but for another reason: cultural misinterpretation.

Craig Storti tells of an employer, Mr. Coyle, giving an employee, Khalil, a performance review. Mr. Coyle gives Khalil high marks in nearly all categories but notes a couple areas for improvement. Mr. Coyle closes by assuring Khalil that there are no serious problems and hands him the written report. Khalil's final comment is, "I'm very sorry to disappoint you, sir."

Middle Eastern societies are very sensitive to shame and to losing face. Khalil has felt the sting of severe criticism even though Mr. Coyle was quite pleased with Khalil's performance and intended no severity. From Khalil's cultural history, any form of criticism is offered with great discretion and usually in an indirect manner. Thus, to have Mr. Coyle state the criticism directly could only be interpreted as severe disappointment. Storti continues:

> We must remember here that Khalil naturally assumes Mr. Coyle is bending over backward to be as sensitive as possible to Khalil's honor. If that is true and this is the best Mr. Coyle can do—if this represents absolutely the best face Mr. Coyle can put on the matter—then Khalil's performance must be very poor indeed.

How, then, should Mr. Coyle have handled the matter? Mr. Coyle's proportions are off; he should have spent most of the interview lavishing exaggerated praise on Khalil and then mentioned any shortcomings very briefly in passing at the end. Even then Khalil would have taken the "criticism" seriously, but, his honor having been preserved, he could have withstood the onslaught. One is reminded of the story of the princess and the pea; even through all those mattresses, she could still feel the rub of the little green offender. In his interview, Mr. Coyle left out all the mattresses.[1]

Mr. Coyle intended the interview to be positive but injured the relationship instead. In the early stages of learning the culture these kinds of things can happen so easily. Good intentions are insufficient when entering another culture. We must also be equipped with the knowledge and competencies to function skillfully.

Among the hardest tasks in life is to divest ourselves of the culture we wear so comfortably. It's like being an actor in a play. Your past life is the "play" you know so well. Everything comes naturally. But all of a sudden, you find yourself in another "play" where all the actors but you know their characters, lines and props. Now you must learn the new "play." It feels unnatural, awkward and even embarrassing—at first. But with a little practice you will be competent and enjoy the play . . . the new culture.

LOOKING AHEAD

This book examines the process of becoming a cross-cultural servant. The information draws from my own experiences, including frequent failures, from the insights of people from many countries who have worked with Westerners, from the extensive body of cross-cultural research and from Scripture, including the Christ who made the cultural transition from heaven to earth to serve you and me.

Part one declares that servanthood must be intentional because it is not natural. We are inclined to serve others from our own frame of reference, but then it is perceived as superiority, cultural imperialism or neocolonialism (chaps. 1-2). Servanthood is a conscious effort to choose one direction and one set of values over another. There is no mystery here. The basic premise is that we have a model of true servanthood in Christ, but we must follow him in his humble servant role, not in his Lord and Christ roles (chap. 3).

Part two describes the process of servanthood. Seven principles constitute the process. The premise in chapters four through ten is that you can't serve someone you do not understand. If you try to serve people without understanding them, you are more likely to be perceived as a benevolent oppressor. Part three deals with implications of servanthood as you exercise leadership and power, or during those mysterious times when God seems to be distant.

The book closes with the Old Testament character Joseph, who experienced all of these situations while staying true to his calling as servant of the Lord.

2

SERVANTHOOD
Choosing the Towel or the Robe

"To hold to a doctrine or an opinion
with the intellect alone is not to believe it.
A man's real belief is that which he lives by."

GEORGE MCDONALD

When God chose to connect with humans, he did so as a servant. It was a most unlikely way to connect, for servants are usually invisible. They wear white uniforms, perform lowly tasks, remain largely silent and, if effective, seem not to be there. People look past them and rarely acknowledge them until needed for a chore. Their rights are few, their power negligible and their status as the dust. Why would Jesus choose to come as a servant? All the images of servant seem so counter-human.

I can think of only one reason Jesus came as a servant: it is the very nature of God to serve.

Were it not so, what hope would exist for humanity? We were hopelessly lost in our sin, unable to render ourselves acceptable to God. Jesus served us by making an eternal relationship with the Father possible through his own life, death and resurrection.

If God connected with us as a servant, that becomes the way we too connect with the people of this world. While it runs counter to our natural desire, we have no choice. We are never more like Jesus than when we serve others.

A subtle but important distinction is necessary. If we set out to become a servant, it can become mechanical and appear artificial or forced. If, however, servanthood is seen as our deepest identification with Christ and inhabits our being, then serving others will be a natural, often unconscious, expression. At this point servanthood is not only what we do but what we are. This seems to be a main point in Matthew 25:31-46. People who served by feeding the hungry, giving drink to the thirsty, providing shelter to the stranger, clothing the naked or visiting the sick and those in prison were apparently not keeping a record of their "servant deeds" but doing what was in their nature. Serving others was their identity.

NOT THE ROBE BUT THE TOWEL

The disciples of Jesus never seemed to get it, at least until it was nearly too late. They envisioned themselves wearing the "robe," enjoying the royal status along with privileges, a big name, prominence and lots of perks. In my embarrassingly honest moments, I find myself too much like the disciples. The "towel," serving others, putting myself out for someone I don't know, thinking of others more highly than myself, putting others' needs before my own, doesn't appeal to me. I prefer being closer to the "throne," nearer the people of power and the place of privilege. We can easily criticize the disciples until we realize that we share deeply their self-centeredness, warped priorities and brokenness.

From beginning to end. The first earthly image we get of Jesus at the very beginning of his life is as a baby born in a barn, surrounded by livestock. The scene announces humility, lowliness, vulnerability, weakness, exposure. The last image we get of Jesus as he ends his earthly life is as a broken body hanging on a cross. The scene communicates humiliation, suffering, failure and, to many, defeat.

Neither the opening nor the closing scenes of Jesus' life suggest anything but a life of humble service—the life of the towel. In between these two scenes are hundreds of others that suggest a kind of towel mission: seeking the lost, performing miracles, touching the poor and marginalized, casting out demons, doing good, teaching kingdom values, nurturing people, praying, fasting and other activities showing his service to humankind. His life was given to carrying the towel, the symbol of humble, obedient and, ultimately, suffering service.

Two metaphors. Two metaphors represent the choice we have every day as we live our Christian faith: a towel or a robe. Both are found in Scripture, but only one is appropriate for Jesus' followers. In biblical times, when a robe was given to another it was considered a special honor (Lk 15:22). When someone was installed into office, the symbol was a robe appropriate to the office.[1]

After three years of being with Jesus, the disciples were still pursuing the robe—prominence and position. Matthew records the story of the mother of James and John approaching Jesus with her two sons and "kneeling down" to ask a favor (Mt 20:20-28). The mother and sons are in this together. She requested the "robe" for her two sons in Jesus' kingdom. She was probably thinking of an earthly kingdom about to be established. She asked for the most powerful positions: one on the right hand of Jesus and one on the left.

The other ten disciples overheard this brazen grab for power and became "indignant with the two brothers" (v. 24), suggesting they were harboring the same vision. Luke notes on this occasion prior to the Last Supper that "a dispute arose among them as to which of them was considered to be greatest" (Lk 22:24).

Jesus censures all of them with one of his more severe reprimands. They are acting like heathen rulers ("kings of the Gentiles") who "lord it over them; and those who exercise authority over them" (Mt 20:25). The lordly model is not for his followers. Jesus alone rightly claims the title "Lord" and shares it with no one. We are not to follow him in his lordly role but in his servant role. The Son of Man "did not come to be served, but to serve, and to give his life as a ransom for many" (Mt 20:28). Greatness is not the goal. Service is the goal, and greatness is defined by Christ in his lifelong exercise of servanthood: "Whoever wants to become great among you must be your servant" (Mt 20:26). For the life of Christ to be reproduced in us, it must be through servanthood, because that is what Christ told us and showed us.

This brief exhortation by Jesus apparently needed visual reinforcement. Only a few days later Jesus demonstrates yet another compelling example of how his followers are to live. His public ministry is over; the shadow of the cross looms. Maybe he recognizes that if the disciples do not grasp this idea of the humble, obedient servant, the future of the church would be bleak. Indeed, there may be no church. In a most unexpected and unforgettable act, Jesus burns the image of humble service into their minds. Here is what Jesus did.

Jesus and the Twelve gathered for the Passover feast, and it was time for Jesus to "leave this world and go to the Father" (Jn 13:1). But he must still make sure the disciples understand one thing: the power of love through living as servants: "He now showed them the full extent of his love. . . . He . . . began to wash his disciples' feet" (Jn 13:1, 5). For whatever reason, no servant had washed their feet as they entered. Foot washing was "generally performed by the meanest [lowliest] servant."[2] Jesus seizes the opportunity by doing the unthinkable: the King of kings and Lord of lords would be the "meanest servant," humbly pouring water in the basin, wrapping the towel around his waist and without a spoken word humbly washing the disciples' dusty feet and drying them with the towel.

After this, he says to them, "Do you understand what I have done for you?" (Jn 13:12). I wonder what went through the disciples' minds. Did they remember "the first will be last" (Mt 20:16) or "whoever wants to be great among must be your servant" (Mt 20:26) or "I am among you as one who serves" (Lk 22:27)?

Next Jesus takes the opportunity, for the last time, to clarify the two roles: the robe—representing the Lord and Christ roles—he shares with no one, for he alone is worthy to occupy it; and the towel—representing the humble, obedient, suffering servant—a role he modeled for us throughout his life. Notice in John 13:13-15 how Jesus distinguishes the two roles for the disciples: "You call me 'Teacher' and 'Lord,' and rightly so, for that is what I am." (Note: he did not say, "for that is what *we* are.") He continues highlighting his other self-chosen role of servant: "Now that I, your Lord and Teacher, have washed your feet . . ." Having separated the two roles, he designates the one and only role the disciples must understand and live: "You also should wash one another's feet. I have set you an example that you should do as I have done for you."

The values of God's kingdom are different from the values of this world. In the world, greatness is judged by the power a person exercises over others. In the kingdom, greatness is judged by service to people. As children of the King, we follow kingdom values.

The Robe and Towel in Cultural Context

Arriving in South Africa, my wife was asked to teach a course on etiquette in the Bible college where I taught. As new and quite naive missionaries, it seemed an acceptable thing. Looking back, my wife is horrified to realize that she taught these black, mulatto and Asian students white North American (and to some degree white South African) etiquette. Her hidden message, revealing a not-so-subtle superiority, was that better people look and act like whites! White etiquette was the standard, and anything less would be inferior. She had unwittingly donned the robe, placing herself and her culture in the superior position. Fortunately other missionaries show us towel Christianity.

Shortly after arriving in northern Sierra Leone (West Africa), Mary realized that when a mother died in childbirth, the child was also abandoned and left to die. One day such an infant nearing death was brought to Mary. But how should she manage it? It occurred to her that feeding the infant could be a community responsibility. So Mary formed a breast-feeding club. She signed up and took her part in the feeding schedule along with other nursing mothers in the community. The child thrived.

Illustrations such as these can alert us to think about the cross-cultural situations we find ourselves in. In the flow of life are we communicating a robe or towel Christianity?

TWO ROLES IN SUMMARY

Jesus came to earth occupying two roles: (1) Lord and Christ, and (2) humble, obedient servant. He alone is Lord and Christ. But he taught and exemplified humble servanthood, the role we are to occupy—the way of the towel. The problem arises when his followers choose to follow him in his kingly role and not in his servant role. They gravitate toward the robe while resisting the towel. The Lord Jesus Christ alone wears the robe. His disciples are to follow him only in his humble, obedient servant role—maybe even his suffering-servant role.

HUMILITY
Posture of the Servant

*"If you ask me what is the first precept of the Christian religion,
I will answer first, second and third, Humility."*

AUGUSTINE

"Humility is the garden of all the virtues."

CHRYSOSTOM

THE MONKEY "SERVES" THE FISH

A typhoon had temporarily stranded a monkey on an island. In a
secure, protected place on the shore, while waiting for the raging
waters to recede, he spotted a fish swimming against the current.
It seemed obvious to the monkey that the fish was struggling and
in need of assistance. Being of kind heart, the monkey resolved to
help the fish.

A tree precariously dangled over the very spot where the fish
seemed to be struggling. At considerable risk to himself, the monkey moved far out on a limb, reached down and snatched the fish
from the threatening waters. Immediately scurrying back to the
safety of his shelter, he carefully laid the fish on dry ground. For a
few moments the fish showed excitement, but soon settled into a

peaceful rest. Joy and satisfactions swelled inside the monkey. He had successfully helped another creature.[1]

The story does not tell us the degree of humility or arrogance the monkey possessed. But, then, that was not the real issue as far as the fish was concerned. The fish likely saw the arrogance of the monkey's assumption that what was good for monkeys would also be good for fish. This arrogance, hidden from the monkey's consciousness, far overshadowed his kindness in trying to help the fish. Thus good intentions are not enough.

Others can't see our motives, only our actions, which become the basis for their impression of us. In like manner, missionaries will need to learn the local cultural patterns so that their desire to serve will be seen as serving and not be misinterpreted. For example, some cultures see assertiveness as a virtue while others may interpret it as pushy and controlling. In the West people start friendships by setting up appointments to meet, but in other cultures such a procedure would signal formality and distance, not friendship.

THE ARROGANCE OF HUMILITY

Humility as found in Scripture often contrasts with the attitude of heroes found in our Western history books. In fact the biblical writers had to invent a new word, *tapeinophrosunē,* to describe the humility God possessed and that should also characterize his followers.[2]

Early pagans held a negative and distorted view of humility. The word described people who were groveling, stingy or mean-spirited,[3] not unlike the view held today in former communist countries (or other totalitarian regimes) where citizens were to serve the leaders by bowing and scraping to the leaders' unreasonable whims.[4] Sometimes the groveling would be motivated by self-interests. In a few instances, though, *humility* carried a meaning closer to that advocated in Scripture. In Plato, for example, the humble person was to be honored, and for a few other writers *humility* was linked with a modest and temperate disposition.

Like all virtues, there are counterfeits. Paul twice warns the Colossian believers about people exhibiting "false humility" (Col 2:18, 23). These people have the appearance of humility but who are driven by their own self-importance. The context would suggest that beneath the surface they feel arrogant in their "superior" knowledge. Some people are seduced by this showy, conspicuous humility and are led astray. Paul warns the believers to beware of this sham. The humility (*tapeinophrosunē*) that God calls for is very different. A proper perspective of the holy God we serve

> *"If anyone would like to acquire humility, I can, I think, tell him the first step. The first step is to realize that one is proud. And a biggish step, too. At least, nothing whatever can be done before it. If you think you are not conceited, it means you are very conceited indeed."*
>
> C. S. LEWIS

brings a proper perspective of self—defined by lowliness of mind, gentleness of spirit and meekness of attitude. These stand in contrast to a haughty, self-important spirit. Paul uses humility to describe the mind of Christ (Phil 2:1-3), and Peter exhorts believers to "clothe yourselves with humility toward one another, because, 'God opposes the proud but gives grace to the humble' " (1 Pet 5:5).

The false teachings in Colossae serve as a warning. Many in the missionary enterprise are well schooled, know Greek and Hebrew, are well versed in the Bible and hold advanced degrees in theology. We support this and praise God for such people. My own biblical education has been extensive. But this good news can also become a challenge—the tendency to believe that we know better than those who have not received advanced degrees. With an unconscious attitude that "my knowledge is superior to yours," I begin to tell you, lecture to you, correct you and have little time left over for listening to you. Usually the people around me will sense this proud spirit. Even though I will call myself a servant and believe I am serving, that is not what will be perceived by others.

I have now become like the monkey without realizing it.

HUMILITY'S MANY FACES

Evangelical author Philip Yancey reflected on the people he most admired—his heroes. He wondered if there was a common trait that made them special. His surprising conclusion: the one important trait they all shared was humility.[5] Yet, Yancey notes, all seemed to possess a strong self-image, held a significant place in their respective vocations and had been credited with worthy accomplishments. What marked them as humble was their "ongoing choice to credit God, not themselves, for their natural gifts."[6] They shared a profound belief that all they were and all they were able to do was by the gracious gifts God had lovingly given them, and the empowering strength of the Holy Spirit.

Humility expresses itself in a near infinite variety of ways, says Yancey. Because humble people are gifted differently and express those gifts according to their unique personalities, peculiar circumstances and natural abilities, humility has many faces.

Humility's face is revealed in the person serving hungry people in a soup kitchen, a teacher taking a student out to lunch, a business person giving the keys of his cottage to the mail room employee for a vacation otherwise unaffordable, the college professor helping the homeless person in the shelter put socks on his swollen feet . . . any gracious act offered with no thought of returned favor or desire to announce the good deed. Such deeds, born of a humble spirit, are usually unconscious because they are embedded as a lifestyle—a natural expression of who they are—much like those noted in Matthew 25:37: "Lord, when did we see you hungry and feed you?"

Yancey's illustrations include young Paul Brand going to India as the first orthopedic surgeon willing to work with leprosy patients; Henri Nouwen, a professor at Harvard, Yale and Notre Dame, finding his greatest satisfaction and education *being with* (not "ministering to," which is different) the mentally challenged at L'Arche Community in France and Canada; and Jimmy Carter, having left the presidency in considerable humiliation, building homes for the poor and now trusted by world leaders to monitor national elections to assure fairness and to initiate reconciliation among nations and groups.

I AM NOT PROUD, BUT I HAVE EVERY RIGHT TO BE

"I am not proud, but I have every right to be" is a phrase playfully used by a friend of mine. To hear some of us talk, that phrase might be the hidden theme of many conversations. We compete in sharing our accomplishments, our newest "toy," the names of powerful friends, our latest international trip or a recent promotion. Dallas Willard's statement, "I have a lot to be humble about" seems far more appropriate. The spirit of Willard's statement implies a proper perspective of self. What do any of us have except by the grace of God? What have we done to deserve his favor? Who among us can guarantee we will be alive tomorrow? Pride has no place in our lives; everything we have is by God's kindness. This perspective will transform relationships.

Humility unites us while pride divides us. The pride of Lucifer broke the unity of heaven and the harmony between God and his creation. Pride continues to break unity between us and God, and between believers. We can't follow Christ as humble servants *and* participate in quarrelsome relationships. The humble servant strives to reconcile people into God-glorifying unity.

Pride, most often expressed as superiority, means someone is either talking up to or down to another person, both of which inhibit open, honest conversation and mutual empowerment. Instead, there is competition. Who is higher? Who is better? Who has more? Who is right? This is "selfish ambition" and "vain conceit" (Phil 2:3).

William Barclay says:

> If a man is forever concerned first and foremost with his own interests then he is bound to collide with others. If for any man life is a competition . . . then he will always think of other human beings as enemies, or at least as opponents who must be pushed out of the way . . . and the object of life becomes not to help others up but to push them down.[7]

Focusing on our own self inevitably leaves little room for attention to others.

Richard Capen was a former U.S. ambassador to Spain and publisher of the *Miami Herald*. He lists humility along with authenticity, character, excellence, trustworthiness and faith as the important values for life. But, "Of all the values at our disposal, humility seems to be the least attractive. You don't see many television ads or billboards extolling the virtues of humility, do you?"[8]

Some people tend to believe that humility is a means to an end—a stage we go through before deserving exaltation. We might be inclined to believe this from verses like "Whoever exalts himself will be humbled, and he who humbles himself will be exalted" (Mt 23:12). Humility, however, isn't temporary; it isn't training for the next level; it isn't a means to some higher end. Humility is a lifestyle, not isolated incidents. It is an attitude toward God, ourselves and others that permeates our thoughts and deeds. The Scripture says it this way: "Clothe yourself with humility" (1 Pet 5:5). When God sees a humble spirit, he may exalt that person. But God expects humility to continue to characterize that person's life. When it doesn't, God will humble him or her.

HUMILITY IS MANDATED, BUT ITS EXPRESSION IS CULTURALLY DEFINED

Humility is a mandated attitude for all believers everywhere; however, the way humility is expressed takes on a cultural face. Perhaps it is the inability to "wear" this cultural face of humility that has prompted many in the world to charge North Americans with superiority or arrogance in spite of our declared efforts to "serve the nationals." The Lausanne Willowbank report, created by Christian leaders from around the world, affirms this perspective:

> We believe that the principal key to persuasive Christian communication is to be found in the communicators themselves and what kind of people they are. . . .
>
> We desire to see . . . "the meekness and gentleness of Christ" (2 Cor. 10:1). . . .
>
> There is the humility to take the trouble to understand and appreciate the culture of those to whom we go. It is the desire which leads naturally into that true dialogue "whose purpose is to listen sensitively in order to understand." . . .
>
> We repent of the ignorance which assumes that we have all the answers and that our only role is to teach. We have very much to learn. We repent also of judgmental attitudes. We know that we should never condemn or despise another culture, but rather respect it. We advocate neither the arrogance which imposes our culture on others, nor the syncretism which mixes the gospel with cultural elements incompatible with it, but rather a humble sharing of the good news—made possible by the mutual respect of a genuine friendship.[9]

TO WASH OR NOT TO WASH

Foot washing in biblical times was one way to show humility. When

Jesus and his disciples entered the upper room, the opportune moment presented itself for Jesus to urge humility yet one more time, but this time he did not use words. I suspect most of the world's greatest sermons are lived rather than preached. My point here, though, is that foot washing was appropriate for its time and may not be appropriate in many of the cultures today. To try to contain humility in a single act is to warp the very idea that humility is an attitude that saturates our entire life. Indeed, humility ought to find expression in every human act.

Millard Erickson offers wise perspective on this point:

> What he was attempting to instill in his disciples was the attitude of a servant: humility and a willingness to put others ahead of oneself. In that culture, washing the feet of others would symbolize such an attitude. But in another culture, some other act might more appropriately convey the same truth. Because we find humility taught elsewhere in Scripture without mention of footwashing (Matt. 20:27; 23:10-12; Phil. 2:3), we conclude that the attitude of humility, not the particular act of footwashing as such, is the permanent component in Christ's teaching.[10]

It is noteworthy that the foot washing was done not just by a servant but by the lowest servant.

One of the great challenges for the cross-cultural missionary is to find those cultural equivalents, or cultural analogies, that express humility. The following chapters will help you discover the ways a new culture expresses some of these biblical virtues. When you have learned and practiced them, you will be able to fit in and communicate more effectively. This process is called contextualization.

Part two introduces a process to help those entering a new culture or ethnicity with the insights and skills that will contribute to positive engagements and long, fruitful relationships with the host people.

SERVANTHOOD
The Process

OPENNESS
Welcoming Others into Your Presence

"This man welcomes sinners and eats with them."

LUKE 15:2

This chapter marks the first distinct step in becoming a servant. I use the metaphor of steps because becoming a servant is a journey—a pilgrimage. While not complicated, the steps require considerable discipline and perseverance to transact in cross-cultural situations because we are only accustomed to servant practices in our own culture. These practices may not translate into servant behaviors in another culture. Calling ourselves or believing ourselves to be a "servant" does not mean that we will be perceived as servants by others.

For those of us who live in or intend to enter another culture, I suggest we postpone naming ourselves "servants" until the local people begin to use words about us that suggest they see servant attitudes and behaviors in us. Humility requires that we hold off making such an important assumption about ourselves until we have some evidence from others. Therefore, let us intentionally, every day, ask what we have learned about how a servant looks and acts in this culture. Otherwise we may be deluded into thinking we are serving when others may not see it that way at all. This way we can avoid being a "monkey." Furthermore, the servant principles in the following chapters will guide us in virtually any relational situation. They certainly would have helped me and my wife navigate the poached-eggs situation.

OPENNESS: THE FIRST STEP OF THE PILGRIMAGE

The steps, as we go through them, may appear somewhat disconnected from each other. They actually make more sense when we go backward—that is, start from the end and work toward the beginning. Here is how it looks starting with the last step:

- *Serving.* You can't serve someone you do not understand; at best you will serve like the monkey.

- *Understanding.* You can't understand others until you have learned about, from and with them.

- *Learning.* You can't learn important information from someone until there is trust in the relationship.

- *Trust.* To build trust others must know that you accept and value them as people.

- *Acceptance.* Before you can communicate acceptance, people must experience your openness—your ability to welcome them into your presence.

- *Openness.* Openness with people different from yourself requires that you are willing to step out of your comfort zone to initiate and sustain relationships in a world of cultural differences.

We will rehearse these steps again in chapter ten, but I hope the overview and logic makes sense to you.

The first principle of servanthood is openness. I say this with some confidence because it grows out of scores of conversations with people from other cultures—but also because there is a wonderful consistency with biblical teaching and what social research reveals. Here and in following chapters I will develop a pattern of offering (1) a definition, (2) relevant biblical teaching, (3) pertinent skills we need to exercise, and (4) a sprinkling of illustrations. While the headings may be different from chapter to chapter, I think you will recognize the pattern.

David Schuringa comments on Luke 15:2:

> Why did it disturb the religious leaders that Jesus ate with "sinners"? To eat with someone is an important symbol of fellowship. And in those days, the Jews had a rule: one is not to have such fellowship with outsiders until they are changed.
>
> If and when outsiders came to repentance, and when they had proven they were sorry by acting like insiders, the Jews could join with them and eat with them—and not a moment before. After all, God's people had no business mixing with unbelievers, right?
>
> Jesus appears on the scene with a new approach. He introduces a brand-new idea. He connects with sinners *before* they repent, before they change, so that they will change. He goes to those who need him even before they know they need him! He seeks out the least, the last, and the lost so that, hearing his voice, they can experience new life. Rather than keeping them at arm's length, he embraces them.[1]

When Jesus welcomed sinners, he welcomed us, embraced us and made us feel safe in his presence.

DEFINITION OF OPENNESS

Openness is *the ability to welcome people into your presence and make them feel safe*. Please reread the definition slowly.

First, being open toward others is an ability, by my definition. This is important because if it is an ability, even if we are not particularly good at it, we can practice and get better.

Second, openness is directed toward people—others like us and, more importantly, others who are unlike us. In Luke 15:2, Jesus, the holy, righteous Son of God, eats with sinners, the despised and rejected—unheard of for anyone concerned with their reputation. To sit and eat with another person indicated oneness with them, solidarity and acceptance—a very countercultural act for Jesus in the Middle Eastern world. God, of course, offers the ultimate welcome to all of us who were once sinners, strangers, aliens. He welcomed us, through Christ, into his presence, and today we enjoy the security of that relationship.

Third, openness must be expressed in culturally appropriate ways so that others feel both welcomed and secure in our presence. This, of course, will mean different things in different places. Recently, a group of Central and Eastern Europeans on a brief study leave in the United States visited Salem Baptist Church, an African American church on Chicago's south side. On average, each visitor reported being hugged about eight times by members of Salem Baptist, who had never seen these European visitors before and probably never would again. Yet the most common response of the white visitors to this all black church was, "We have never felt so welcomed."[2] Even though the worship style was unlike theirs, they felt (and enjoyed!) the warmth and goodwill of the Salem people.

Hugging, even of someone you just met, is common in Latin America and other cultures. In South Africa I was shocked to see an Afrikaans father kiss his adult son on the lips as a regular morning greeting. The cheek kiss is more common in some cultures, and it is done every time a person is met, even if several times a day. However, in much of Asia, touch is not often used as an expression of welcome. Thus a bow is preferable to the hug or handshake. Most Asians are quite familiar with the Western handshake and are reasonably comfortable with it. But why not try to discover how Asian friends (new and old) greet each other and then fit into their cultural patterns—a good practice for any culture you happen to be in? But the kind of welcome I am suggesting goes far beyond the greetings.

Practicing openness in the new culture will require that we change. Miroslav Volf uses the term *embrace* when speaking of welcoming others into our presence. Then he says, "The will to give ourselves to others and 'welcome' them, to readjust our identities to make space for them, is prior to any judgment about others, except that of identifying with them in their humanity."[3]

NON-CHRISTIANS AND CHRISTIANS

Recently my wife returned from seeing our son and daughter-in-law in California. We both had much to talk about. One of her early stories had to do with two meetings she attended. The first related to a film location where our son was acting in a short movie. When she arrived on the set, the movie crew, mostly younger, figuratively embraced her, drew her in, engaged her in conversation, probed her history and made her feel welcome (openness!). She felt like a valued and instant member of the film crew. In fact, one crew member called her "Mother." The whole evening was a celebration of her and each other while also accomplishing the tasks at hand. Sounds like a wonderful evening with a group of Christians, doesn't it? Yet, with the exception of our son and his wife, none of them knew Christ as far as she could tell. Nevertheless, my wife called it one of the highlights of the trip.

The following evening she went to a small Bible study with our son and daughter-in-law. While she was introduced to everyone, no one asked a single question about her during the entire evening. It was as if she had become invisible. She almost felt like an intruder. As the evening wore on she made one comment during the Bible study but no one picked up on it. The stunning contrast to the previous evening caused her to think about the difference between the two groups—how differently each reacted to her presence and how she felt. In one she felt warmly received, valued and accepted as one of the group. In the other she felt like a stranger, excluded and distant. Why did she feel so much more comfortable with the apparent non-Christians? It was their openness. They opened their hearts and lives to her, and made her feel safe, like family.

Surely the Christians in the Bible study group would be horrified if they knew how they were perceived by my wife. Certainly it was not intentional on their part. So what caused one group to beautifully embrace her and the other to seemingly ignore her? Think about it. Then think about some recent experiences you have had where a stranger entered your home, your group, your clique. How do you think the person felt when he or she left?

THE CROSS SIGNALS GOD'S OPENNESS

The cross may be the single greatest symbol of openness. On the cross Jesus' arms were open wide. In his dying breath he still signaled his openness to receive those who would come to him in repentance. But it is not only an openness to those who wish to repent of their sins but also to us who wish to draw near for comfort, peace, refuge, hope and grace. Openness is grounded in the very nature of God.

Openness is also captured in the biblical concept of hospitality. The apostles Paul, Peter and John all mention hospitality (Rom 12:13; 16:23; Tit 1:8; 1 Pet 4:9; 3 Jn 8). Twice it is listed as a requirement for church leaders. Why is this virtue so powerful in Scripture? In North America, hospitality conjures images of inviting someone, usually friends, neighbors or relatives, into the home for a meal, perhaps overnight. Showing hospitality and providing a meal seem synonymous, especially toward friends or relatives. Yet the Scripture expands the idea considerably.

Hospitality refers to an attitude that prevails in a person's lifestyle, an attitude of extending grace to people, including the stranger, the person who is different. It certainly includes inviting people to your home, but if that is the extent of it, we have missed the core meaning. Hospitality is extending love to those we don't know and who may be of a different ethnic or cultural history. It is the idea of being gracious to all people, welcoming them into your presence and making them feel valued. A true servant is characterized by hospitality—one who welcomes and embraces those who are unlike us—just as Jesus embraced us across our radical differences.

Hospitality is rooted in the word *hospital,* which comes from two Greek words meaning "loving the stranger." It evolved to mean "house for strangers" and later came to be known as a place of healing. Eventually, *hospitality* meant connecting with strangers in such a way that healing took place. Therefore, when we show openness toward people who are different from us, welcome them into our presence and make them feel safe, the relationship becomes a place of healing. As we welcome people just as they are and invite them to join us just as we are, it becomes a sacred event reflecting what Jesus did for us—providing us with a healing relationship.

In the Company of Angels

Stephen Rhodes says:

> The most important virtue any church can embody is the virtue of hospitality. Because God has welcomed us, we are called to welcome others—and not because it is the nice and polite thing to do, but because it is the holy and just thing to do. Scripture warns that our unwillingness to be hospitable may cause us to miss out on a divine encounter. As the letter to the Hebrews advises: "Do not neglect to show hospitality to strangers, for by doing that some have entertained angels without knowing it" (Heb 13:2). Simply put, we have to welcome and be gracious to everybody, because we can't be sure who the angels are.[4]

Being open, hospitable and gracious is warranted for another compelling reason: when we "touch" another human being for good or ill, we "touch" God himself. Matthew 25:31-40 records Jesus' story of the sheep and goats, a most dramatic story because it metaphorically deals with life and death. To the sheep, who represent the believers, Jesus says, "Come, you who are blessed by my Father; take your inheritance, the kingdom prepared for you since the creation of the world" (v. 34). The stunning reason for the sheep entering the Father's eternal kingdom is: "For I was hungry and you gave me something to eat, I was thirsty and you gave me something to drink, I was a stranger and you invited me in. I needed clothes and you clothed me, I was sick and you looked after me, I was in prison and you came to visit me" (vv. 35-36). To me these are examples of being open—graciously responding to people around us as an unheralded lifestyle, not as something special or extraordinary.

Equally astonishing was the response of the "sheep" (the righteous): "Lord, when did we see you hungry and feed you, or thirsty and give you something to drink? When did we see you a stranger and invite you in, or needing clothes and clothe you? When did we see you sick or in prison and go to visit you?" (vv. 37-39). They had no idea that these acts of everyday kindness toward others were touching Jesus himself.

Jesus' striking response to their bewilderment is, "I tell you the truth, whatever you did for one of the least of these brothers of mine, you did for me" (v. 40, see also v. 45). When we touch others in gracious ways (with God's grace) we are touching God himself! Therefore, every act toward other human beings is either a sacred or profane act. It either treats them with dignity or it dehumanizes them. We have no other choice.

PROFANITY

Every human contact requires an openness that invites others into our presence for a moment of grace, if we so choose—or a moment of profanity. Yes, that is the right word. We profane another person whenever we fail to honor them as human beings. Because every human being is made in the image of God, each is intrinsically connected to him and is therefore sacred, being stamped with God's own imprint. How I treat "the least of these" is how I treat their Creator. If I extend to them hospitality, I reveal God's beauty and grace. If I am uncharitable toward another person, I fail to honor the God who gave them dignity. Jesus' identification with us is so intense that whatever touches us touches him. And whatever I do to another human, I do to him. By profaning another person, I profane God. Thus the greater profanity may not be cursing, bad as that is, but failing to extend openness and hospitality to another person who bears the Creator's image. "He who oppresses the poor shows contempt for their Maker" (Prov 14:31).

Perhaps the family metaphor will clarify this further. I am a father. My children bear, in part, my image. We are connected. You touch my children, for good or ill, and you touch me in the same way. The same is true for my wife and grandchild. In whatever way you touch them, you also touch me. God has created us all, and in that sense we are his family—his family in creation. He is our Father in creation. He has shared his image with us. He is connected to each of us. Touching one of his own is touching him.

Stephen Rhodes summarizes so powerfully:

Hospitality, when you get right down to it, is unnatural. It is difficult to place others first, because our inclination is to take care of ourselves first. Hospitality takes courage. It takes a willingness to risk. But as our Lord reminds us, if we only love those who we are sure will love us and welcome those who will welcome us, then we have done little to share the love of God, for as Jesus says, even the heathen do that.

You see, most of us know what true hospitality feels like. It means being received openly, warmly, freely, without any need to prove ourselves. Hospitality makes us feel worthy, because our host assumes we are worthy. This is the kind of hospitality that we have experienced from God, and all that God asks is that we go and do likewise, particularly to "the alien among us."[5]

Exhibiting a spirit of hospitality creates an atmosphere of safety and security whereby deep, meaningful conversation can blossom. In doing so we affirm people as human beings and speak peace to their inner being. We also signal that there is One who extends hospitality to all people and who can satisfy our ultimate need. Cultural differences, however, tend to interfere with staying open and extending hospitality toward others.

OPENNESS AND HOSPITALITY

Showing openness and extending hospitality is not a one-way street. Being a gracious receiver may be equally important even though those extending generosity may have much less. The following illustration makes this point:

> When I was doing campus ministry, a Mexican American student leader in our InterVarsity chapter expressed concern about his mom, who had just had surgery. I suggested that we buy her some flowers and he would take them to her and let her know they were from his Christian friends at school. When I saw him the next week, I asked how his mom had responded. His face fell. "You know, she was really embarrassed to get flowers from people she didn't even know."
>
> I was disappointed, but I thought quite a bit about it and realized that to try to start a relationship by giving wouldn't work. That was focusing on her need and weakness, and she and the family probably had way too much of that already as working-class Mexicans within the Anglo-dominant American culture. We didn't have an already-established relationship between us that would allow reciprocity. So I told Eduardo that I'd really like him to ask his mom—after she had recovered—to invite a couple of us over for

dinner. For Christians it seems counterintuitive, but I realized that we should meet her in a receiving posture that would affirm her dignity by honoring something she had to give.

It took a while, but eventually there was a family barbecue, and Eduardo invited another student and me. I took my guitar and played and sang a couple of Latin pop songs I had learned as a teenager in Colombia. Eduardo's mother and aunt, as it turned out, were very musical and knew lots of songs—and they started singing. I put down the guitar and just listened in delight. I'll never forget sitting in their driveway as they stood next to the grill, heads thrown back, singing *rancheras* in harmony. And the food was delicious!

I have realized since that this is very biblical. After all, when Jesus ate with people, he was usually *their* guest. We sometimes honor others most by receiving their kindness and hospitality and music rather than by trying to give to them.[6]

Cultural Differences and Staying Open

Dichotomizing—the Western tendency to see things in discrete categories—shows up in our desire to quickly know where things fit. When we have labels on things, we can manage them. One of our favorite ways to dichotomize is in the area of "like me" or "unlike me." If something is like me, then it is in the "good" category. I approve. I move closer to it. I promote it. I have positive feelings about it. If something is unlike me, I respond with suspicion, distance, frowning, critiquing and trying to change it (or change *you*) to look like me.

A while ago I read a study about how quickly American people like me make decisions about other people. The study measured how quickly people made judgments about other people when they first met. Imagine you and I were standing in line somewhere and you, in a friendly way, turned around and introduced yourself to me. How long do you think it would take me to determine if there was a possibility of friendship between us? Thirty seconds? A minute? Five minutes? How long?

The surprising result: it took the average person between 2.4 and 4.6 seconds to decide if there was a potential for a relationship.[7] (Two things about this should be noted: usually the decision is unconscious, and given time and opportunity, we may change our mind.)

Two other points from this study are relevant for us regarding openness. We categorize other people (and their cultural practices?) very quickly and very unconsciously. Once we have them categorized, often negatively, we close our mind about them. Then our behavior follows, also unconsciously. That is, what happens in our head in less than five seconds influences the future of that relationship. Efficiency may not be a virtue in the area of relationships.

More frightening: on what basis do we make that quick judgment? The decision can only be based on a visual scan of the other person. Like an electronic scanner, our eyes instantaneously survey the other person. We observe the physical makeup: skin color, height, weight, clothing, accent and maybe smaller features like skin texture, hair style, nose size or ear shape. We judge primarily on surface characteristics. Isn't this stereotyping? I gather three or four bits of appearance data about you, and in less than five seconds I determine whether I am interested in a relationship—whether you are worthy of a relationship.

THE BAD NEWS GETS WORSE

Imagine again that you and I are in waiting in line and you, wanting to be friendly, turn around and strike up a conversation. In less than five seconds I have already placed you in a category—let's say I'm not interested in a relationship (don't take this personally; it's my problem). Let's say further that your hair and overall appearance are disheveled. You look like you just got out of bed and picked your clothes from the bottom of a pile. Now something else also tends to happen. Not only have I already decided there is no future in this relationship, but I decide that you are undisciplined or disorganized or a social misfit or weird or . . . whatever pops into my head.

I have made a second judgment about you. I assigned to you negative attributes: undisciplined, disorganized and so forth. When people don't speak or look like what we prefer, we assume negative things about them. In the social research, this is called "negative attribution."[8] Negative attribution, in essence, states that whenever we hear, see or experience someone or something that confuses us, we assign him, her or it a negative characteristic. We blame the person or thing for our confusion. It seems to be a universal human trait, but people in the United States, where the research was done, may do it more quickly than others.

AMERICANS MEET GERMANS

Occasionally I have been a corporate consultant. In a large automotive company, German engineers met with American engineers to cooperate on a joint project. Each group was asked to share their perspective about the others. Even though this was their first meeting, comments were honest and revealing. When the lists were made, the overwhelming number of perceptions each held about the other were negative. Compounding the problem, both groups believed their negative perceptions to be true, not just stereotypes. Consequently, both groups entered this relationship with suspicion, resistance and predetermined negative characteristics about the other.

Stereotypes, whether based on past experience or learned from others, tend to close us off to being open toward members of another group. When we categorize another group of people, it's usually negative, and then negative behaviors invariably follow.

Not only do we make two-to-five-second decisions about whether people are like us or dissimilar to us, but we somehow feel free to also name the negative things about them. This tendency can be a major problem when entering another culture where people (1) look very different, (2) their environment is very unlike ours, (3) they have a different language or accent, and (4) they live in ways that confuse us. By God's grace, there is a better way. And with the power of the Holy Spirit we can learn to practice skills that will move us beyond these natural but ungodly tendencies.

SKILLS FOR OPENNESS

For each of the steps to servanthood I have identified a set of skills. While awareness of these skills helps, they are useless unless practiced. The skills are such that they can be practiced in the home, church, stores, school or neighborhood. Practicing these skills in your home culture will make them more natural, so when you enter another culture, you will not need to develop them, but only find the appropriate ways to express them. This book introduces the attitudes and practices of servanthood across cultures, but you must actually apply the ideas in your own culture first.

Suspending judgment. The first skill necessary for developing an attitude of openness toward others who are different is the ability to *suspend judgment.* Suppose I am standing in a store waiting to pay the cashier. An unkempt woman with ungroomed hair, sloppy dress and neglected hygiene stands behind me. In less than five seconds I will probably draw some conclusions about this person, none of them positive. Yet if I catch myself and analyze my thoughts, I might reconsider. Maybe she just learned her father has cancer and is rushing to help him. Maybe her sick child desperately needs medicine. Or maybe she's depressed. Or carefree. By suspending judgment, I can keep my mind open to alternative explanations for what I see and hear rather than immediately assuming something negative. The issue is not so much what might have caused her appearance but what is my response to this "stranger" whom God has created. If I allow negative attribution to take over, I am inclined to ignore the woman's humanity and her true needs. But if I stifle a quick response and remain open, it becomes an opportunity for hospitality—a moment of grace, maybe even healing.

Attribution theory says we quickly and unconsciously think negatively about others if, in some way, they do not measure up to us or our expectations. We then assume the attribution to be fact—before checking it out. The Bible calls this "judging others." When Jesus was accused of violating the sabbath, he declared, "Stop judging by mere appearances, and make a right judgment" (Jn 7:24). Not all judgments are wrong, but most premature judgments are. We must suspend judgment until we see more clearly. That is unnatural and takes time. This is why we must practice suspending judgment.

Making a judgment is the same as coming to a conclusion. If the conclusion is wrong, we have acted unjustly toward the person. Furthermore, once we have formed a conclusion, our mind is closed to new information that may change our conclusion. Even worse, once our conclusion is formed, we tend to see only the evidence that confirms that conclusion. In a new culture, faced with a multitude of differences, we are prone to judge from our cultural perspective. Too often we see negatively what God sees as difference. If it is merely different and not wrong, we should stay open and be accepting.

We all struggle to keep our judgments impartial. We are rightly cautioned by God to judge only with extreme care because to misjudge is to damage another human being and thus touch Jesus with the same disregard. *Suspending judgment,* therefore, is the first skill in maintaining an open attitude. It keeps us from premature negative judgments. It also keeps us open to new information that may help us judge accurately.

The following are some steps you can take to avoid premature negative judgments:

- Recognize you are making a negative judgment. It will serve you well to be able to monitor these kinds of thoughts in virtually every social situation. Ask yourself, *Am I jumping to a negative conclusion?*

- Stop as soon as you recognize you have a negative thought or make a negative remark or negative judgment. Ask whether you have enough information to be negative about that person. Should you suspend judgment, get more information and seek cultural understanding before drawing a conclusion?

- Does the observed behavior violate some clear mandate of Scripture or should it be labeled as a cultural difference?

- If it violates a clear biblical mandate, how can you respond so that you still communicate openness while addressing the concern? This takes great wisdom and should not be done quickly and probably not in the same way as in your own culture.

- Unless you are a veteran of several years in a given culture, I would strongly urge you to share your thoughts with a mature local pastor or an experienced missionary rather than tackle it yourself.

- If, however, you are concerned about something that is a cultural difference, then you may remain open, even celebrate it as a part of God's wonderful diversity. Then try to understand how this difference is part of the larger tapestry of the culture.

Practicing these steps in our home culture will contribute to better communications, fewer misunderstandings and stronger relationships with siblings, parents, spouse, in-laws, children and colleagues. Notice I did not say friends in the above list. The reason is that with friends we usually practice positive attribution. That is, most of what they do we cast in a positive light.

Anytime we evaluate another culture from our own cultural perspective, the other culture is likely to look worse. We generally favor our own cultural perspective and believe it to be superior to other perspectives. Such ethnocentrism often causes us to assign negative attributes to the things we observe. Those negative categories interfere with our ability to show open, positive regard toward others. Not everything will be positive about the new culture, but at least for the first couple of years you should exercise negative attribution with caution. The apostle James offers help: "My dear brothers, take note of this: Everyone should be quick to listen, slow to speak" (Jas 1:19). Perhaps by listening we might learn something that will keep us from the grievous error of misjudging someone.

Tolerance for ambiguity. A second skill necessary for openness to function effectively is *tolerance for ambiguity*—a prominent topic in the cross-cultural communication literature. Tolerating ambiguity, or living in uncertainty for periods of time, taxes our emotional strength, which in turn drains our physical capacity. Most Westerners manage their lives using PDAs, daily planners or computer pop-up reminders. Little room remains for the unexpected or ambiguous. We work hard to avoid uncertainty and to live an ordered, predictable life. The unknown, the unexpected, is an unwelcome intrusion in our schedule. We believe it to be dangerous to the order we have built into our existence.[9]

During times of ambiguity we want things to clear up, we want answers, we want understanding, we want resolution, and we want it *now*. Some of us don't perform well during times of uncertainty. There are, however, two compelling reasons why we should exercise patience, keep the anxiety in check and patiently endure the difficult time: (1) God wants us to know that he is in control of our lives and will act in love toward us at all times even though it may not seem so at the moment; and (2) God wants us to learn through this experience, to grow us in some important way. Practicing patience during times of ambiguity in our home culture means the skill will be available for us to cope with the ambiguities of the new culture.

When entering a new culture, ambiguities press upon us at all times. Sometimes we feel like hiding. A temporary escape may help sometimes, but usually we get better at handling the discomforts by hanging in there, keeping an open mind, processing our observations and asking questions. Slowly the pieces of the cultural puzzle will fit together and a beautiful picture will emerge from the confusion. Tolerance for ambiguity allows us to persevere when criticizing or running away is what we would prefer.

Thinking gray. Steven Sample, president of the University of Southern California, notes a third skill for promoting openness: *think gray.*

> Thinking gray is an extraordinarily uncommon characteristic which requires a good deal of effort to develop. But it is one of the most important skills which a leader can acquire. Most people are binary and instant in their judgments; that is, they immediately categorize things as good or bad, true or false, black or white, friend or foe. A truly effective leader, however, must be able to see the shades of gray inherent in a situation in order to make wise decisions as to how to proceed. The essence of thinking gray is this: don't form an opinion about an important matter until you've heard all the relevant facts.[10]

Get the information before making a judgment. Monitor your thoughts as you experience new people, places and situations. Stop those fleeting thoughts and name them. Analyze them. Are they negative? Positive? True? Have they been tested for accuracy? In most cases you can think "gray" and not force a premature judgment.

Positive attribution. The fourth skill to practice in developing an attitude of openness is *positive attribution.* Whereas negative attribution assumes the worst about the others when we are lacking certainty, positive attribution assumes the best, while not being naive. I am inclined to quickly think negatively about others. This serious flaw has handicapped me over much of my life, especially in initiating and building early stages of relationships. One thing that has helped me is traveling extensively. The people of the world have been kind, gracious, open, trustworthy and generally wonderful to me. Slowly I have made some significant changes by intentionally thinking the best about them. Then, if necessary, I may notice some of the less pleasant things.

A side effect of my tendency to see the negative in other people is that I then judge the whole person (or group) by that one negative. I generalize from one characteristic to the whole person. Of course, this is grossly unfair. I am the big loser because I might have learned and grown so much from the people I stereotyped. While we should not overlook a person's weaknesses or pretend they are not there, neither should we cast that person aside for one weakness. Positive attribution keeps us open toward others, allowing for a stronger relationship.

Paul encourages us to think about the good, the positive: "Whatever is true, whatever is noble, whatever is right, whatever is pure, whatever is lovely, whatever is admirable—if anything is excellent or praiseworthy—think about such things" (Phil 4:8).

REFLECTION ON MY EXPERIENCE

Nearly forty years of observation suggests to me that my (older) generation has tended to reject cultural diversity because we have not adequately distinguished it from religious diversity. We have tended to mix our culture and Christianity quite easily, quite comfortably and with little critique. Often confusing cultural differences with religious differences, we have judged cultural differences as wrong. In recent years the opposite seems to be more true. The younger generation, perhaps influenced by postmodernism and the general relativism of society, has been less inclined to distinguish between cultural and religious differences. They often prefer to see both as valid choices. Thus the younger generation blurs religious and cultural issues, tending to believe if peoples' hearts are sincere, whatever their religious convictions, God will accept them. Both tendencies have their dangers, though they are not the same. My own sense is that the two generations need to converse, moderate each other's extremes and in doing so move closer to where God is.

Having made this statement, I tend to affirm the relational priorities I see in the younger generation. They don't see people as a means to an end, as objects for their witness or as sinners to be conquered. Rather, they place genuine value on building strong relationships and letting witness grow out of life together. In many ways the thoughts of this book will connect more directly with these values.

A RESTRICTION ON OPENNESS

While openness is a wonderful virtue, it is not to be misconstrued as religious relativism. Hopefully, you have sensed this throughout the chapter, but I want to be intentional in stating it. Our challenge is to be inclusive in extending grace to all people yet exclusive in affirming that the Bible is the authoritative truth of God. While this often brings charges of exclusivism, narrowness, rigidity and elitism, the fact is that to make the Bible only one of many truths is to destroy its claims. It negates its value and authority, turning it into a good piece of literature among many other equally good pieces. Thus religious pluralism or religious diversity denies the distinctiveness of the Bible. Failure to speak to the unique claims of Christ has serious consequences. Stephen Rhodes quotes Lesslie Newbigin in saying, "Relativism which is not willing to speak about truth but only about 'what is true for me' is an evasion of the serious business of living. It is a mark of a tragic loss of nerve in our contemporary culture. It is a preliminary symptom of death."[11]

At the same time, we should not reject cultural diversity, because it is born of the natural differences that exist in people. We can remain open to the cultural diversity as long as it doesn't violate a clear mandate of Scripture. Openness to cultural differences will lead us into acceptance, the next step in being a cross-cultural servant.

5

ACCEPTANCE
Communicating Respect for Others

"We have just enough religion to make us hate,
but not enough to makes us love one another."

JONATHAN SWIFT

"If we do not accept as good, God's shaping of our person and
life in our own culture, we will never be able to accept his
work in the lives of others who are culturally different from us."

SHERWOOD LINGENFELTER AND MARVIN MAYERS

We could argue that *acceptance* and its opposite, *rejection,* are among the most powerful behaviors in the human race. Think about it. Haven't many of your devastating life experiences come from feeling rejected—no longer accepted? Fired from your job? Divorced? No longer part of the "in" group? A broken relationship? Shunned? Cut from the team?

On the other hand, many of your cherished experiences probably are a result of feeling completely accepted—one of the group, trusted, secure, respected, wanted, valued, desired. "Nearly all of us have a need to be accepted by others," says Carley Dodd.[1] Life is good when we feel accepted.

A CULTURE OF REJECTION

Dallas Willard offers a stinging critique of Western culture and its institutions:

> The infant who is not received in love by the mother and others is wounded for life and may even die. It must bond with its mother or someone in order to take on a self and a life. And rejection, no matter how old one is, is a sword thrust to the soul that has literally killed many. Western culture is, largely unbeknown to itself, a culture of rejection. This is one of the irresistible effects of what is called "modernity," and it deeply affects the concrete forms Christian institutions take in our time. It seeps into our souls and is a deadly enemy to spiritual formation in Christ.[2]

Children and teenagers tend to express exclusion rather blatantly. We see it in youth fashion—someone wearing discount-store clothing is mocked and made to feel unacceptable in the halls of school. Several television specials have dealt with the serious problem of bullying in the elementary schools—older or bigger children intimidating and beating up other children. Reading the accounts of school shootings, Columbine, for example, we learn about the rejection that fueled the anger which drove the perpetrators to their crime. Adults inflict rejection on others as well, but usually with more "sophistication." Acceptance, rooted deeply in the character of Christ himself, must be more prevalent in our relationships if we are going to grow into his likeness. So what does *acceptance* mean, and how should it affect us as we minister cross-culturally?

Acceptance is *the ability to communicate value, worth and esteem to another person.* As in chapter four, we will look at supporting biblical concepts, ideas from the social science literature and the skills necessary to be accepting people.[3]

ACCEPTANCE BEGAN WITH GOD

Romans 15:7 states, "Accept one another, then, just as Christ accepted you, in order to bring praise to God." These are God's challenging words. The passage makes four major points. First, what does it mean that Christ has accepted you? Consider the alternative: Christ has rejected you. Our acceptance by Christ and our acceptance of others has enormous implications for all of life.

In class I ask my students: "What does it mean that Christ has accepted you?" Their inspiring responses include

- Jesus took the initiative in accepting me; he took the first big step toward establishing the relationship with me.

- He accepted me without any conditions, not based on my performance; in spite of my sin and weaknesses, he accepted me just as I was.

- His acceptance of me is forever, no termination point.

- Because he accepts me, I am secure, no fear of exclusion or dismissal.

- He sees me as a person, without ethnicity, gender, nationality or social status labels.

- He valued me enough to give up his life; accepting me cost him dearly.

- "While we were still sinners, Christ died for us" (Rom 5:8) expresses God's profound acceptance of us, the degree to which he valued us, and his desire for a relationship with us.

ACCEPT ONE ANOTHER

The second major point of Romans 15:7, and the most difficult for me, is to "accept one another"—with the standard being: "just as Christ accepted you." It was written to believers in Rome who were not getting along very well. They were bickering over differences, with each group believing its position to be more spiritual than the others' (see Rom 14). Paul wants them to apply this concept of acceptance to cut through the false feeling of superiority and restore love and unity to the body of Christ.

Given the list above, here is how accepting one another will look:

- We are to take the initiative in showing acceptance toward others, making them feel valued and respected.

- We unconditionally accept others without considering their external features, lifestyle, decisions, habits and so forth. (Note: acceptance is not approval.)

- We do not have the option of rejecting any person, though we may, in a culturally appropriate way, address behaviors that the Bible clearly declares as sinful.

- We are to eliminate our own dehumanizing behaviors such as threats, intimidations, power-plays and other ungodly forms of manipulation.

- We accept people—period; like Jesus, we must reject labels such as race, generation and gender as defective guides for how to treat another human being.

- We expect that accepting others in these ways may cost us dearly.

The third major point connects acceptance of others with the glory of God. Something amazing happens when the people of God become accepting people. It reveals the glory of God. Here is the lesson for all who work cross-culturally and belong to Christ. Accepting one another may be among the most powerful acts of love we can offer to each other because it promotes oneness. Oneness in Christ is so wonderful that the natural expression is to sing the praises of God. The world notices the healing love and wholeness of the body and sees a great and mighty God. They see his glory.

Fourth, accepting each other promotes the mission of God. When we accept one another across our differences, it promotes unity in the body. This unity reveals the glory of God and the power of his love. In this atmosphere, says Paul, mission happens: "So that the Gentiles may glorify God for his mercy. . . . [T]he Gentiles will hope in him" (Rom 15: 9, 12). If Satan can cause dissension among Christians, nothing of significance will be accomplished. For this reason, accepting one another becomes absolutely central to the mission God has given us!

TROUBLE IN THE CHURCH

Differences in the churches in Rome and Corinth caused people to take sides, and fellow believers were either "in" or "out" (1 Cor 1:11-13). Paul labels these differences as "disputable matters" (Rom 14:1)—gray areas. Disputable matters are issues that should not be cast as right or wrong, good or bad, moral or immoral. Nor should we look down on someone who believes differently regarding these disputable matters (Rom 14:3). Holding differing opinions on the same issue should not break our fellowship. In Rome and Corinth the issue was food—what may or may not be eaten. Those with a weak conscience would refrain from some foods while others, including Paul, believed that "all food is clean" (Rom 14:20; cf. Rom 14:14; 1 Cor 8:8). But the bottom line is, "Stop passing judgment on one another. . . . Do not destroy the work of God for the sake of food" (Rom. 14:13, 20). Then comes an ominous warning: "When you sin against your brothers in this way . . . you sin against Christ" (1 Cor 8:12). I wonder how many of us realize mistreatment of another believer is a "sin against Christ?"

Paul closes his discourse on a positive note. An accepting Christian values the other person so highly that he or she would rather sacrifice a personal preference, even a right, than risk losing the relationship or being a stumbling block to that person (1 Cor 8:13).

TO ACCEPT IS TO BLESS

Blessing, a major theme in the Old Testament, is way of communicating acceptance. To bless someone is "to bow the knee" before them as a sign of honor and respect.[4] Even more importantly, blessing means "to highly value someone or something."[5] The Scripture portrays blessing in relational terms: God blesses people, people bless each other, and people bless God. Rhodes comments:

> In the Bible, by blessing humankind, God is telling us how highly he values us. When we bless one another, we remind one another how important and significant our lives are to each other. And when we bless God, as in worship, we are telling God how important [he] is to us.[6]

The church in a multicultural world is called to bless the nations by valuing persons and cultures in their particularity. God calls us to remind the world of the high value and worth God has placed not only on each person but on each family, ethnicity, tribe, tongue and nation. We not only pray for the well-being of persons, but we also seek to be in relationship with them. Therefore the ministry of blessing can never be an ethnocentric affair; it must be a family affair, as in "all the families of the earth."

God's blessing of Abraham in Genesis 12:1-3 informs us that the point of our being blessed is to bless others; that is, having discovered how highly the Creator values us, we are in turn to value God's creation. The ministry of blessing reminds us of the essential connectedness of the Christian life. It reminds us that we were created to live in relationship. We cannot live alone, counting our own blessings. Rather, the act of blessing affirms God's multicultural intention for creation. In blessing and being blessed, we discover the reestablishment of the true unity willed by God.[7]

Some of us remember the old hymn "Count Your Blessings," which encourages us to "see what God hath done." Perhaps we ought to add another verse encouraging us to bless others by telling them of God. In blessing others, especially those who are outside our normal relationships, we bless God.

DIGNITY: THE SACRED ENDOWMENT

God created humans "in his own image, in the image of God he created them; male and female he created them" (Gen 1:27 TNIV). People everywhere bear God's image. His likeness appears in you, me, the person down the street, the poor person, the inner-city person, the HIV/AIDS-infected person and even the person on death row. God has been generous. He has shared something of himself with every human being that makes the person absolutely unique—unlike any other creature. God wants us to see *his* face as we look into the face of others.

Since we bear God's image, no one is insignificant; no one is worthless. Life has meaning, and we have meaning and importance because God's own imprint is upon our humanity. Thus we must see others as God sees them, treat them as he would and name them as he names them.

Unconditional, continuous acceptance then is based on the fact that God has bestowed dignity and worth on every human being. Thus we have no choice. Either we treat them with the respect and dignity that God has given them or we profane God's image in that other person by treating them with less value. We cannot honor God and at the same time treat another person in a manipulative, dehumanizing, disrespectful way. As Darrow Miller says, "How you treat a person in the brief moment when you pass together through a revolving door tells the world what you believe about them."[8] Our view of people can be seen even in the most insignificant circumstances.

That's not a prostitute. In the mid-1990s my wife and I, both teaching at a Christian college, were feeling out of touch with the needs and realities of the world. At the invitation of John Green, a graduate student, we decided to minister to people by walking the streets of Chicago one night a week for about a year. Mark Van Houten and John Green, veterans in this ministry, oriented us to street life. Walk slowly so people can approach you. Walk near the curb; alleys can be dangerous. Walk the same route each night so you become familiar to those on the streets.

Read the gang symbols so you know whose turf you are on. Cross the street rather than walk around a group of people that might threaten you. We would arrive at about 8 p.m. and slowly walk the same route each week, finally heading home about 3 a.m.

Walking with Mark one night, I noticed a lady at the corner ahead. She was scantily clad. I turned to him and said in a voice the lady would not hear, "Is she a prostitute?" He paused; I remember thinking, *Why the pause? It's obvious.* Then he said firmly, "No! That's not a prostitute. That's a *person* . . . in prostitution." His profound statement affects me to this day.

When I saw this woman, I saw a prostitute. When Mark saw her, he saw a human being.

What do you think Jesus would have seen?

What made the difference in our perceptions? I tended to categorize people—homeless, drunk, drug addict, prostitute, pimp, panhandler—then I would know how to treat them: respectable vocation brings respect; disrespectful vocation brings disrespect. I decided who to accept not by the fact that they were made in the image of God but by the kind of life they were living. Mark, however, saw the image of God in everyone in spite of their activity. This truth made everyone first and foremost a human being loved by God, accepted by Christ, sacredly endowed with dignity and worthy of being treated with respect and honor by every other human being. He accepted this person in prostitution just as Christ would.

Over my dead body. Over twenty-five years ago, *Christianity Today* published an interview with Helmut Thielicke, a German pastor who resisted the Nazis and survived the Holocaust. The article focused on "how the terrible things perpetrated by Hitler could ever have happened in a country which brought forth Bach, Beethoven, Thomas Mann and other luminaries of art and science."[9]

Thielicke gives eight reasons but then declares the "the ultimate reason why all of this could have happened is theological in nature," and it lies in the defective anthropology of the rulers. He explains, "There are two extremely different views of man." On the one hand the person is evaluated according to "his functional worth. . . . [T]his view of man is pragmatic." When someone is no longer able to function because of age, handicap, or injury then this "worthless life, like a machine which no longer functions, must be scrapped. In this case the term used is 'liquidate.' "[10]

The opposite view is the one we find in the gospel. Here the dignity of man rests not upon his functional ability, but rather upon the fact that God loves him, that he was dearly purchased, that Christ died for him, and that therefore he stands under the protection of God's eternal goodness. And the mentally defective and those who are worthless in the eyes of men are also under his protection.

Thus Bodelschwingh, the director of an institution for epileptics, could fling himself against the myrmidons of the SS and say: You will take them away (for killing) only over my dead body. He knew that even the most wretched of them, in whom our human eyes can scarcely see a spark of humanity, are loved by God—and no one dares to snatch them out of his hand. They have no immanent functional values but they do have what Luther called man's "alien dignity," which means that they have a relationship, a history with God, and that the sacrifice of God hallows them and makes them sacrosanct. Only in this "alien dignity" is there any security. In any other case we are delivered over to human evaluation and manipulation.[11]

Whereas the Nazis saw the epileptics as worthless, like worn out machines, this German director saw them as sacred, human beings worthy of acceptance and honor.

Nudging people toward one of two destinies. C. S. Lewis provides us with a summary of how to see people and puts a profound perspective on every human contact. In his sermon "The Weight of Glory," he says we are inclined to think too much of ourselves and too little of our neighbor.

> It is a serious thing to live in a society of possible gods and goddesses, to remember that the dullest and most uninteresting person you talk to may one day be a creature which, if you saw it now, you would be strongly tempted to worship, or else a horror and corruption such as you now meet, if at all, only in a nightmare. All day long, we are in some degree, helping each other to one or other of these destinations. It is in the light of these overwhelming possibilities, it is with the awe and circumspection proper to them, that we should conduct all our dealings with one another, all friendships, all loves, all play, all politics. There are no *ordinary* people. You have never talked to a mere mortal. Nations, cultures, arts, civilization— these are mortal, and their life is to ours as the life of a gnat. But it is immortals whom we joke with, work with, marry, snub, and exploit—immortal horrors or everlasting splendors.[12]

Today, every contact I have with another person becomes either a sacred or profane moment depending on how I see it and handle it. To accept and affirm the dignity of the other will nurture the image of God in them. To devalue that person or fail to show respect will contribute to a further distortion of the image of God in them.

With ease, it seems, we look down on others who are poorer, less educated, mentally or physically challenged, of lower status, or in some other way different from us. It appears to be a human problem since the poor or less educated may also demean others.

FACTORS LIMITING OUR ACCEPTANCE OF OTHERS

Language. In a cross-cultural situation, language limits our ability to verbally communicate acceptance to others. This makes things more difficult. To make no effort to learn another's language is by itself a form of rejection of people. We cannot separate ourselves from the language we speak. It is how we define ourselves and make meaning out of life. Not to know my language is not to know me. Even when short-term missionaries make an effort to learn at least some greetings and a farewell, it communicates that they value others.

When my wife and I lived in South Africa, we occasionally journeyed north into Zimbabwe (then Rhodesia), the land of her birth, the home of her missionary mother and the burial place of her father. The first time we entered Zimbabwe we stopped for gas, and a black Zimbabwean served us. I spoke to him in English (probably his third language after Ndebele and Shona), and he dutifully attended to our car. My wife got out of the car and greeted him in Shona. A huge smile lit up his face and his body quickened with joy. Never have I seen such an immediate transformation, all because a white person spoke his language. He felt accepted—valued.

Impatience. Impatience limits acceptance of others. I like to see things happen quickly, the sooner the better. I hate waiting in lines; TV commercials frustrate me because they make me wait for the rest of the program. Long stoplights are irksome wastes of time. I know I can pray and do other productive things during these wait times, but often the impatience is too consuming. In many parts of the world waiting is a nonissue. Meetings don't start on (Western) time; appointments run thirty to forty-five or more minutes late; traffic can be snarled forever; roads are bad, requiring hours to make relatively short journeys. All of this can be very frustrating but only because it's not what I am accustomed to. We need to find ways to deal with life's little frustrations, or they will hinder our ability to value and celebrate people.

Several things help me. I have become a people watcher, which is both intriguing and informational. Observation is a wonderful way to learn another culture. After observing others, try to name the values that you see them living out. I also carry reading material. Scripture memory cards are useful when I have extra time. Starting a conversation with someone who seems not to be too busy can be an unexpected delight. I have been known to do stretching exercises and light aerobics if I think I can get away with it. If impatience is a problem for you in your home culture, you will have your patience tested often in a new culture. Without several strategies to deal with daily frustrations, you will build up negative feelings, and people will sense rejection from you, aborting any opportunity for meaningful ministry.

Ethnocentrism. Ethnocentrism is an unconscious hindrance in communicating acceptance. It refers to the tendency of every person to believe that their own cultural values and traditions are superior to those of other cultures. The more the other culture is unlike my cultural background, the more I am inclined to make unfavorable judgments.

While ethnocentrism is a human trait, it seems Americans reveal their ethnocentrism more quickly and more assertively because they are more forthright with their thoughts. This may be why many people from other cultures think of Americans as arrogant, controlling and even neocolonialistic. Most Americans who travel cross-culturally, often for humanitarian purposes, are quick to identify a problem, offer a solution and then get on with fixing whatever they determine is wrong. They love to be efficient and good stewards of time and resources. They find satisfaction in a job well done for others who are "needy." Typically seen as virtues in the United States, these "virtuous" behaviors can be perceived as aggressive and paternalistic elsewhere, making others feel inferior, weak, defective or disrespected. Consequently, the good we intend may not be seen as good by those we serve. And the blessing that flows from acceptance isn't felt.

The typical American response is "Why didn't they tell us? They should say something if we aren't doing it right." There is a good chance they did tell us in ways that were "loud and clear" for their culture. But we Americans were unable to hear them because of our cultural tradition.

For example, people from many cultures use stories to communicate their attitude or opinion on a matter. If you heard a story from a local person that you thought was quaint but you weren't sure why they told it, you might assume it was intended for *you,* to provide you with insight about the culture so you would understand and grow in sensitivity.

Category width. The range of things we place in a mental category is called category width.[13] We all have mental categories by which we organize the world, make decisions and avoid confusion. These categories help us distinguish between trucks and chipmunks, telephones and golf balls, people and light bulbs. We name everything in our world, and those names become the categories by which we think. The person with wider categories can accept a broader range of items in a category. The person with narrower categories would rather create a new category than expand a present one.

For example, a wide-category person might put more things into the "cultural differences" category, whereas a narrow-category person would not be inclined to stretch existing categories and instead would put many of the differences into the "wrong" category, which already has many other items in it. The narrow categorizer has tighter definitions of "right," "wrong" and "different." You can see how quickly this can cause conflict between missionaries and between missionaries and nationals. Our mental categories and how we use them determines how we interact with others.

Both types of people possess some wonderful strengths, so it isn't a matter of which is better. However, when it comes to cross-cultural adjustment and ministry, a person with narrow categories has some tendencies that could hinder relationships. For example, narrow categorizers tend to be more ethnocentric, more reactionary and seek less information before forming judgments.[14] Wider categorizers, on the other hand, tend to seek more information before making judgments and are more likely to put cultural differences in a neutral category rather than in the "wrong" category.[15] This means that some of us must exercise more caution before making a judgment, lest we err in ways that are unfair to the local people.

Dogmatism. Dogmatism refers to the degree of rigidity with which we hold our beliefs, our cultural traditions, our personal preferences. The dogmatic person, one who holds firmly to their own beliefs and traditions, tends to see difference as wrong or inferior which must be corrected. This person lacks "openness in communication because of rigid boundaries of belief or practice . . . in a culture."[16] After being around a dogmatic person very long, one can feel put down since there is no room for exploration of ideas or dialogue. Conversations usually become win or lose confrontations.[17] Dogmatic people can easily burn relationships and sometimes are downright obnoxious. They talk as through their way of seeing things is the only way. If you don't see it their way, you are wrong. Thus dogmatic people often exhibit defensive communication that brings out defensiveness in other people. They can be argumentative, but they claim they are so in an attempt to find or defend truth.

It's one thing to have wider or narrower categories, but it's quite another to hold them as absolutely and always right. "The rigid mind cherishes sharp, clear-cut distinctions."[18] "If we hold our categories rigidly, we do not recognize individual variations,"[19] and once we have placed someone (or some idea or tradition) in a category, we are unlikely to change our mind in spite of the evidence.

When to be dogmatic and when to be flexible. Some things require dogmatism, especially when we have confidence in the Bible. The Bible speaks authoritatively about a number of things, but we should not be dogmatic about all things. For example, I am dogmatic about such core doctrines as the triune Godhead, the deity and bodily resurrection of Christ, salvation by faith in Jesus Christ, the virgin birth, the absolute integrity of Scripture. While I'm not open minded on these matters, I am willing to discuss why I believe and hold firmly to them. I also want to listen carefully to those who disagree with me. In all situations I want my discussion to be heavily seasoned with graciousness and sensitivity— some call this an "irenic spirit."

I have opinions about other doctrines but am also open to other views—things like church government, the time of the Great Tribulation, the ways people worship, even the mode of baptism. I may hold firmly to a doctrine but hold loosely to the way it is expressed—this is called the "fixed flexible" principle. For example, God calls all his people to gather for worship. That is the fixed part. But he doesn't dictate the style of worship. That is the flexible part. The Bible offers guidelines like prayer, Bible-centered teaching and preaching, and God-focused music and praise. God gives latitude for how we worship as long as the people of God focus on him, his worthiness and his claim on our life.[20]

However, there is a subtle tendency for me to believe that all my beliefs are indisputable and all my cultural traditions best. I slide easily into judging you from my cultural, personal or theological perspective. When we find ourselves acting pompous and dogmatic in such situations, we do well to remember the words attributed to Martin Luther: "He who believes his doctrine to be perfectly right and true has only to lift his hands and touch his ears and discover they are the long furry ears of a donkey." Take care not to grow donkey ears.

Meeting the Russian bear. I have had my own struggles with narrow categories and dogmatism. As I was growing up, Russia (i.e., the Soviet Union) was seen as the great threat to freedom and democracy. Periodically the fear of a Russian attack would be so great that my elementary school would conduct air-raid safety procedures. The bell (we had no sirens) signaled us to slip out of our desks and crouch under them or proceed to the basement, where brown barrels of dried foods and drinking water assured us we could survive. As a child I learned to hate the Russians, never having seen one or met one. I knew they were all evil, destructive people. This may be a difficult to imagine in contemporary society, but the cold war had this affect on many of us.

In 1990, soon after the Iron Curtain fell, I was asked to conduct a number of conferences with universities in the former Soviet Union countries. My first thought was *Why? Why should these people who caused me, my family and my country so much fear now be treated favorably? The bottom line? Can I show respect and value those who I still place in the category of enemy? Can I accept them as Christ does?*

We met at Moscow State Linguistic University. The theme, chosen by the Russians, was "Building Character Through Higher Education." I took four Christians from universities in the United States and one from Australia who could speak to this topic from a Christian frame of reference but also sensitively so as not to offend our Russian hosts. The Russians had an equal number of professors presenting papers. We made clear in advance that we believed in the God of the Bible. One must draw standards of conduct from somewhere and that is where we based our beliefs about building character. This seemed to cause no disruption.

The conference proceeded smoothly although quite formally. Relationships were pleasant but stiff. Interactions were frequent but also guarded. The banquet on the final evening proved to be a turning point. I had a growing awareness that these people were not only Russians but human beings. They showed us courtesy and respect in a number of ways, which I received with outward gratitude but also hidden suspicion of their motives. Yet I could not deny the cumulative effect. The beautiful display of food, drink and decorations evidenced their appreciation for our time together. The protocol called for various leaders of the conference to make short speeches and offer a toast. I did something that surprised me.

I found myself recounting my history of crawling under the desk, marching to the basement, sensing imminent danger and strong dislike for the Russians. The dignitaries around the table, the president (called the rector), his cabinet, department heads, all sat in studied silence as I poured out my feelings. My colleagues, stunned at my brutal honesty, wondered if I was going to destroy whatever good will had been built.

Then I began to recount the wonderful hospitality of my Russian counterparts—how they had dismantled my stereotypes and fears. I thanked them for the gift of kindness to me and that I could no longer believe they were my enemy. Based on our week together, I expressed my hope for our two nations to peacefully coexist, maybe even finding friendship. I committed myself to sharing the story of this place, where former enemies found each others' common humanity and discovered we were more similar than dissimilar. All of us wanted to live our lives free of threat and destruction. We wanted to enjoy our children and grandchildren without the ominous cloud of war and devastation shadowing each day.

The rector stood and offered his toast and response. Reflecting deeply, obviously probing his own range of emotions, he recounted similar fears, animosity and sickening resentment toward the Americans. The Russian government emphatically communicated to their people that the Americans were intent on destroying Russia. The American military machine was poised to launch a surprise attack to destroy their country, their children, their future. The regular newspaper reports of imminent annihilation by the Americans brought him intense anxiety while robbing him and his loved ones of a peaceful life. It was a deeply moving disclosure.

Then, with shifted tone, he began to tell us jokes that Russian people created about their own government and military. Now we laughed together and found yet another piece of shared humanity. Concluding, he said that if nothing else happened except this exchange at the banquet, the whole conference would have been a success. But there was far more that was accomplished, and he wished his American guests peace and prosperity. He gave us gifts, invited us back as soon as possible and expressed hope for the future based on our experience here.

The event had become a powerful lesson to me about putting people in rigid categories and dogmatically believing that I was right and didn't need to change. God patiently broke down my narrow, rigid categories and helped me to see the Russian people as he sees them—valued, image-bearers, loved and accepted by him. The enemy had become persons to be treated with respect and dignity. As the rector finished his speech, he turned and gave me a hearty hug—the Russian display of acceptance.

Then an insight came to me with force. When I was an enemy of Christ, he died for me. Now his words take on new meaning: "But I tell you: Love your enemies and pray for those who persecute you" (Mt 5:44).

ACCEPTANCE OVER EVALUATION

Social research says that the most frequent response Americans make to a situation is to evaluate what they just saw or heard as right or wrong, good or bad.[21] Usually the standard for such judgments is how similar or dissimilar it is to me and my beliefs. We often use ourselves as the norm by which to measure others. If they measure up, we accept them; if not, we try to change them (one form of rejection) or distance ourselves from them (another form of rejection).

It's a good idea to monitor our thoughts and words to see how often evaluative language is part of our daily lives with our spouse, parents, children, friends, supervisors, subordinates—all our relationships. Consider a few examples: I like or dislike; I approve or disapprove; I am drawn toward or shun; this is right or wrong; it's acceptable or unacceptable, cool or uncool, nice or mean, attractive or unattractive, favorable or unfavorable. You get the idea. Try monitoring your thoughts and words, and see how many are evaluative rather than affirming, descriptive, inquiring or expressing empathy.

When my wife received her Ph.D. from Michigan State University, our teenage son was heavy into the Indiana Jones look, talk and behaviors. At her graduation we were taking pictures of her adorned in the beautiful doctoral regalia. Our Indiana Jones impersonator swaggered up next to her for his picture. He put his forearm on her shoulder, leaned against her with his legs crossed and wide-brimmed Indiana Jones hat appropriately cocked on his head. I took the picture but quietly, on the side, asked my wife if we should ask him to take a "normal" picture with her since this would be our record of this significant occasion. (Note my evaluative comment that this was unacceptable.) She was wise in her response: "No, let's not do that. I think some day we will look back and laugh at this moment." She was right. I evaluated and was ready to say to my son, "Your style is not acceptable to me. Please change it for a minute." My wife chose a wiser path. Today we laugh when we see the picture and fondly remember it without regret.

Anthropologists Sherwood Lingenfelter and Marvin Mayers make a similar point in a cross-cultural context: "One of the biggest problems . . . is that we often insist that others think and judge in the same way we do. We do not accept one another in love, but rather we try to remake those around us into our own image."[22] That inclination to remake others in our own image is cultural cloning. People end up looking more like us than like Christ. Acceptance of them in their own cultural traditions helps us move from cultural cloning to discipling into the image of Christ. Servanthood means helping people look more like Christ, not more like us.

SUMMARY

The first principle in the pilgrimage to servanthood is *openness*. To be open like Christ is to invite others into our presence and treat them in ways that will make them feel safe in our presence. Second, *acceptance* of others is to proactively communicate respect and dignity to each human being based on the fact that each is an image-bearer of God. Both openness and acceptance are deeply rooted in the character of Christ and expressed in his relationship to all humanity. The third principle, *trust*, moves us yet closer to the goal of servanthood. Without trust little of significance will be accomplished.

TRUST
Building Confidence in Relationships

"The most important step in entering a new culture is to build trust.
Only when people trust us will they listen to what we have to say."

MARVIN K. MAYERS

"No task is more important in the first years of
ministry in a new culture than the building of
trusting relationships with the people."

PAUL HIEBERT

Relationships travel best over strong bridges of trust. Think back on your strongest relationships—maybe a friendship, a good marriage, a parent-child relationship. How did those relationships become strong, rich, meaningful and significant? Can you describe their importance to you? What roles have they played in your life? Have they always been smooth? If the relationship continues to the present, what is it worth to you? Have you built strong trust with someone of another ethnic group or nationality? Or is everyone you trust from your own culture?

LESSON FROM THE MENTAL HOSPITAL

Robert Greenleaf, a former AT&T executive, has given considerable thought to public and private institutions, including the church. Greenleaf writes about a visit to a state mental hospital where about fifty people were kept in a locked room. He mused, "These patients were sullen and hostile looking. They were standing or sitting as isolated beings with no apparent interaction among them." Because Greenleaf observed only two orderlies in the room, he asked the staff psychiatrist about their safety. Greenleaf wondered if the patients might gang up on the guards. The staff psychiatrist responded, "Not a chance; those orderlies are quite safe. You see, it is part of the illness of those poor patients that they cannot get together on anything."[1] As long as the members of the church are unable to work together, the world is safe from the church's influence.

Trust binds us together, and we function best when that bond is strong.

To Trust and Be Trusted

Definition. Trust is *the ability to build confidence in a relationship so that both parties believe the other will not intentionally hurt them but will act in their best interest.*

This chapter explores the idea of trust—how we can build trust with the people around us, particularly people who are different from us. In most cultures of the world, trust is the glue that holds relationships together, the oil that reduces friction, the energy that promotes spirited cooperation. Without trust, relationships grind slowly if not indifferently. If we trust someone, we cannot be indifferent. Deep trust drives us to act in the best interest of the other. Think about it. Don't you act more responsibly and enthusiastically when someone you trust will be affected by your actions?

Ingredients of trust. For trust to grow it must be nurtured in several ways. First, trust takes time. Instant trust rarely exists. That would be a naive or pseudo trust. Trust comes in small, incremental steps over time. Through a variety of experiences we evolve into a more comfortable, confident relationship. This is even more true when we don't know the language of the local people. Learning their language actually signals your desire to know these people and build relationships of trust.

Second, building trust requires risk—mostly emotional. Testing strengthens trust. Friendships grow while working through difficulties together and finding resolution. This includes clarifying misunderstandings, admitting wrong, apologizing and forgiving. As we deal with the bumps in a relationship, mutual confidence increases. Soon both parties are confident the other will not intentionally hurt them.

Third, trust must be built from the other person's perspective. Let me illustrate.[2] For our first anniversary I gave my wife snow tires. As a male growing up in rural Wisconsin, it would have been a gift that I would have appreciated. Such a gift would have increased my trust in the giver. However, I made the mistake of believing that what would build trust with me would also build trust with my wife, who was more metropolitan and was born and raised in a warm climate. She had no clue about snow tires. So we had a cross-cultural and cross-gender "situation." Had I asked the question, What will build trust from *my wife's perspective?* I would have come up with a very different gift: flowers, jewelry, perfume or a piece of pottery she had admired on an earlier shopping trip. The snow tires—well intentioned, expensive and necessary for our car—did not communicate love and trust. But the snow tires did communicate insensitivity, thoughtlessness, self-centeredness, lack of care—you get the idea. I was like the monkey who tried to serve the fish by taking it out of the water. Trust must be built from the other person's frame of reference.

Fourth, trust must be nurtured. Strong confidence in a relationship beautifully portrays the Trinity; absolute trust exists between the three distinct persons of the Godhead. The Trinity is the model for marriage, family, church and other relationships. For example, in marriage, two people say, in effect, I trust you so much that I want to spend the rest of my life with you. Even more, I intend to do everything I can to bring you security, happiness and fulfillment. Divorce happens when trust has been so badly broken that it seems beyond repair. To keep trust strong, both parties must regularly ask, What will build trust with this person (or this group)?

GOD AND TRUST

He trusts us. Our grounding for trust rests in God's character. He trusted us. But when? how? and why? Some answers to these questions will guide us in thinking about trusting others who are different from us.

Trust finds its roots in creation. God created every human being and entrusted us with his own image (Gen 1:27). Imagine God giving us something that makes us completely and wonderfully distinct from the rest of creation. His image bestows on us such dignity that we are loved by him above all other parts of creation. With God's image imprinted within our nature, we have been given the privilege of choice, the exercise of will. With this will the Creator allows us to love him with all our heart, mind and soul, or to despise and profane him. We are allowed the choice to do good or evil.

In creation God also trusted us with managing his world (Gen 1:28-30). He has made us vice regents over his creation to care for the world he has given us—a global responsibility.

God builds trust. I believe one of the reasons for the miracles God performed in the Old Testament was to earn the trust of his people, Israel—so they would have faith in him rather than in false gods. Such displays of power were intended to show Israel that he, the Lord God, was trustworthy for all aspects of their life. By word and deed God declared to his people, "Trust me. I am worthy of your complete, unwavering confidence, regardless of your circumstances. All other gods are untrustworthy. They will betray you, but I will never betray you."

Another staggering act of trust was the incarnation—God entrusting his Son to us. God, who was not visible to the people of the Old Testament, was now made visible in his Son Jesus, who was human (Jn 1:14;

Phil 2:7). God built trust with us by sending his only Son to live among us. The holy, righteous Son of God entered sinful humanity to show us God and to invite us to a relationship with him. Jesus' displays of power over disease, demons, ailments and even death are signs that he is who he says he is: the Christ, the Son of the living God. Therefore, trust him with your life and your eternity.[3]

Perhaps the greatest act of trust was Jesus giving his life for rebellious humankind—a righteous person giving up life for his enemies (Rom 5:7-8). In his ascension Christ entrusts us with his life and mission, that is, to live out his life in the world, to be his light in the darkness, his mercy to the needy, his justice to the downtrodden, his voice declaring he is "the way and the truth and the life" (Jn 14:6). In Jesus' own words, "I tell you the truth, anyone who has faith [trust] in me will do what I have been doing" (Jn 14:12).

Another act of trust is God forgiving our sins. When we repent of our sins and ask God's forgiveness, he promises to forgive us (1 Jn 1:9). In our repentance, we are telling God that we have broken trust with him. In his forgiveness trust is renewed and the relationship is restored. As his servants we follow this pattern: forgiving one anther when trust has been broken in order to restore the relationship. Living in unforgiveness is refusing to live like Christ.

Yet one great act of trust remains: the resurrection. As the disciples faced a confusing present and an unraveling future, they found Jesus words reassuring:

> Do not let your hearts be troubled. Trust in God; trust also in me.
> In my Father's house are many rooms; if it were not so, I would
> have told you. I am going there to prepare a place for you. And if
> I go and prepare a place for you, I will come back and take you to
> be with me. (Jn 14:1-3)

Jesus says, "Trust me all the way to the resurrection."

In the Old Testament Joshua proclaimed, "Not one of all the LORD's good promises to the house of Israel failed; every one was fulfilled" (Josh 21:45). The God of Scripture, the God we love and serve is absolutely trustworthy. God's own trustworthiness inspires us to trust him and to extend that trust to others who also need to experience the God who can be trusted.

BUILDING TRUST ACROSS CULTURES

In cross-cultural experience, trust is even more important but also more difficult for several reasons. First, trust is built differently in different cultures. Most people build trust somewhat intuitively, without thinking. Stop and think about how you build a new relationship with someone: a new neighbor, a new church member or someone new at school or work. What do you do to build and maintain trust?

Some of the things we do in American culture will work in other cultures: smiling, phoning, e-mailing, spending time together and showing interest. However, some things that build trust in one culture may actually undermine trust in another culture. For example, you are in a new culture and decide to get to know someone better—to build trust. You agree to meet at a certain place, but the person arrives twenty minutes late. Lateness for a meeting usually undermines trust for Americans.

> *"It is a greater compliment to be trusted than to be loved."*
>
> GEORGE MACDONALD

Suppose the person from the new culture begins to ask you how much you paid for your shoes, house, jewelry or tennis racket. You wonder why the preoccupation with money. These questions undermine trust in your home culture. Or let's say the relationship with the other person is going smoothly, and you, a male, are pleased with the trust that is emerging. Then, out of nowhere, the other person, also a male, takes your hand and holds it while walking down the street. Males holding hands with males?

What does this mean? Does it mean the same thing in this host culture as it does in your home culture? How can you find out?

Trust is culturally defined. Some activities may build trust in both cultures, but don't assume this. In most cultures being late isn't disrespectful; it's a way of life and most people think nothing of being fifteen, thirty or even more minutes late. Lateness should not be seen as a violation of trust. What about the preoccupation with money? People are curious about different things. Often people in less wealthy countries are awed by the wealth in the West and find it intriguing.

Some Vietnamese may tell you how much they paid for the gift they are giving you. Then they explain in detail the effort they made to acquire it just for you. Telling you the cost and effort is their way of saying how much they value their relationship with you. It's their way of building trust. Money, how you talk about it and the exchange of gifts can be tricky if you are settling into a culture for a longer period of time. It is best to get some wise local advice, or you can injure relationships without intending to—just by doing your cultural thing.

Handholding, especially within the same sex, has certain connotations in the West. When it happens in another culture, we are inclined to interpret it from our own cultural frame of reference. In most cases, though, it is a sign of good friendship, revealing a level of trust. The same would be true for walking with arms across each other's shoulders or arms interlocked at the elbows. Trust-building is culturally defined. Learn how it is done in the culture you will be entering so that you can accurately interpret others' signals and you will be less likely to offend them with yours.

Trust is fragile. In my earlier years I would not have placed trust very high on my priority list. Experience has changed my thinking. Without trust friendships, families and organizations, including the church, sink into dysfunction. People with experience can attest to this. Richard Capen has found trust to be one of the essentials in life. He comments,

"Trust is absolutely essential in everything we do—trust in marriage, between friends, at work, in public life. . . . Without trust we are doomed to chaos and confusion because nothing can work."[4]

As human beings we must connect with each other in order to survive. Our inability to value cultural and ethnic diversity increases the complexity of building and maintaining trust. Yet God wants that diversity to be respected and harnessed in such a way that together we strive for the glory of God and unify around the work of his kingdom. "Make every effort to keep the unity of the Spirit through the bond of peace. There is one body and one Spirit—just as you were called to one hope when you were called—one Lord, one faith, one baptism; one God and Father of all, who is over all and through all and in all" (Eph 4:3-6). The prerequisite for such oneness is: "to be completely humble and gentle; be patient, bearing with one another in love" (Eph 4:2).

Why these scriptures, and why all this talk about trust? One reason: trust is fragile. It breaks easily. One day a friendship is strong, then one person does something the other was not expecting and trust is shattered. When broken it takes time and effort to rebuild. We have all experienced this. When immersed in cultural differences, we can break trust without even knowing it. Therefore, we must have a strategy for repairing it: forgiveness.

FORGIVENESS: REPAIRING BROKEN TRUST

Every relationship experiences times of broken trust. Sometimes it's minor, such as not showing up on time; sometimes it's major, such as violating the sanctity of marriage. When trust is broken, most want to repair it, especially if the relationship is important. Only one thing can restore broken trust: forgiveness—forgiveness sought and forgiveness received.

Westerners often transact forgiveness through a verbal exchange. One party says, "I am sorry for what I did (or said); will you forgive me?" The other party usually responds, "I forgive you." With this brief transaction, the relationship is restored and is free to grow again, assuming both parties are sincere. Based on Matthew 18:15-17, many in the West believe the only way to resolve conflict is through direct confrontation, face-to-face; it's verbal, one person telling another what he or she has done wrong.

In most parts of the world seeking forgiveness the Western way only makes the situation worse.[5] Shame, honor and saving face are core values in other cultures, and when violated, the relationship usually breaks. Forgiveness will repair the damage, but it must be contextually understood.

Forgiveness in Sudan. A few years ago a colleague and I went to Khartoum, Sudan, to teach on forgiveness. After lunch on the second day, laboring under intense heat and watching that glazed look come across the eyes of these dedicated pastors and church leaders, I decided to take a risk. I had to get them engaged—talking—something that would keep this from becoming a forgettable moment. I asked the group, "How do you do forgiveness?" Several responded matter-of-factly, "We say 'I'm sorry and will you forgive me?' Then the other party usually says, 'I forgive you.' "

"Does this work?" I asked. Many shook their heads negatively while others simultaneously uttered no. "What do you mean?" I probed. Now the glazed looks were gone and everyone seemed alive in spite of the smothering heat. One said, "Well, we say the words but nothing changes." Others supported his lament. "Where did you learn to do it this way?" I asked. "From people like you, Westerners," came the quick response. A look of betrayal spread across the eighty faces crammed in a room designed for forty. I looked through the windows full of black faces peering in from the outside. Their expressions also seemed to be saying, "We did what you told us, but it doesn't work." Exchanging words of forgiveness doesn't bring a reconciled relationship. Instead, they got more of the same distance and alienation. What was wrong?

The next hour would be transformative in my thinking. I was feeling energized by being among a wonderful but very different group of people. We were learning together, from each other, with each other. We had moved, unconsciously, back to our core identities—human beings struggling with how to live together.

"How did your fathers and mothers, grandfathers and grandmothers respond to conflict situations?" I inquired, hoping this might prove fruitful. The room erupted in hands shooting up to answer the question. Several told their stories. The one I share was from a person of the Dinka tribe in southern Sudan, though most of the stories had common elements.

The Dinka person, now at the front of the room, began to speak with eloquent passion.

His parents and grandparents did forgiveness differently. To begin, people didn't try to solve their conflict the way the West does, by face-to-face confrontation, speaking directly about what each other did or did not do. Instead, a mediator would be called in, a person of stature, fairness and discernment. The mediator would go first to one party and try to establish a base of understanding from that person's perspective. Then he would do the same with the other person.[6] The mediator would ask questions and continue this process until he began to sense that one or the other or both wearied of the brokenness and now longed for a restored relationship.

In collectivistic or communal societies, when two people are alienated from each other, that alienation extends to the other members of the immediate family and often to the extended family, including what we call in-laws. It may spill over to the entire clan. Thus broken trust may disrupt life in the entire community.

Eventually one person will hint, maybe intentionally, maybe not, that things were better before the conflict. The mediator then goes to the second person and says something like, "I think so-and-so misses the days when you were friends." Hearing this, the second person says something like, "Really! It is sad that it has come to this. People should be able to get along with one another." Armed with this sentiment, the mediator returns to the first person and communicates the sadness felt by the second that people can't get along.

The mediator begins to see changing attitudes and signs of openness, and with these comes the potential for embrace. When he senses the spirit of forgiveness in both parties, he calls for a feast. He delegates each family to bring the various dishes. The party that may have been at greater fault will bring the meat, the "ram," as the Dinka person described it. A neutral place is designated.

The family bringing the "ram" arrives earlier, builds the fire and begins cooking. The other family arrives and all joyously enter the preparations for a great festival—great because it marks the beginning of a new future, a better future. The mediator arrives, and when all is ready he washes his hands in the gourd of water. Others do the same in descending order of importance, children going last. As they gather around the food, the mood is celebratory and the families mingle in happiness. Near the end of the meal, after several hours, the mediator stands and moves toward the fire. On the way he picks up the gourd of water, dirtied by so many hands, and pours it over the fire. The mediator turns over the stones on the perimeter of the fire to cover the ashes. Then he gives an admonition: "Let him be accursed who turns over one of these stones again."

Of course, he is speaking symbolically. The fire represented the conflict that had "burned" and destroyed a valued relationship and alienated families. The water represented the forgiveness that emerged in their hearts and replaced the fire of conflict. The stones rolled over to cover the smoldering ashes symbolized the finality of forgiveness; we are not to dig up the old hurts and revisit them. Forgiveness means we never go there again.

Other world cultures. When I returned to Trinity Evangelical Divinity School, where I teach, I immediately gathered as many international students as I could find. About fifteen students came, curious about my agenda. I rehearsed the story of the Dinka person. Then I asked the group, "How do your parents or grandparents do forgiveness? When trust is broken, what is the process by which they rebuild trust and restore the relationship?"

Over the hour, most spoke from their cultural contexts, which included Asia, Africa and Latin America. Common themes emerged. In every situation a mediator helped resolve the conflict and restore the relationship. Mediators function in many important roles in most of the world, though they are relatively uncommon in the West. One important role for the mediator is to resolve conflict with fairness while protecting honor of both parties. Wisdom and patience are required to accomplish this delicate procedure.

Another theme also emerged. Extended families would get involved in reconciliation. When two people came into conflict, the affected families often put pressure on the warring parties to fix the problem; often spouses couldn't talk with each other because they were on opposite sides. Some children were forbidden to play with others because they were connected with the "wrong" family. Social events couldn't be attended if the other person or family would be there. Life became miserable for everyone.

In the West conflict may not affect the wider circle of family and friends as much, although some ripple effect may occur. Typically, in our individualistic culture, we believe conflict to be an individual matter. "It's *your* problem" is the frequent response. In most of the world, especially if there has not been significant exposure to Western culture, the response is, "It's *our* problem."

One last common theme relates to celebrations. The African students at Trinity Evangelical Divinity School resonated with the feast for the extended families. Those from Latin America said that once forgiveness has been transacted through the mediator there would be music, drink and dance. The Asians present spoke more in party terms but with the intent of celebrating the end of a dark piece of the past and the arrival of a better day.

In the West forgiveness is a verbal exchange. In the majority of the world, forgiveness is an attitudinal and behavioral change usually by celebration with food. Nearly always the outcome is reconciled relationships that function effectively, often better than before the broken trust.

A CAUTION ON TRUST

Sometimes trust can be misplaced; we simply shouldn't trust someone who is not trustworthy. Sometimes trusting someone too much too soon is naive. Trust doesn't replace good sense. For example, when a known sex abuser, even a repentant one, is nearby, a healthy skepticism and extra caution with children is simply wise.

How trust is built, violated and rebuilt in a given cultural context will vary. Thus you will need to discover for yourself what breaks trust and how trust is restored in your particular situation. You will need to learn this from the local people. But they won't tell you until they feel you are trustworthy. Trust becomes the basis for deep sharing and mutual learning. Out of this we discover how to serve. But how do we pursue such learning?

7

LEARNING
Seeking Information That Changes You

"A missionary friend of mine once said,
'Things were simple before I went to Africa.
I knew what the African's problem was, and I knew the answer.
When I got there and began to know him as a person,
things were no longer simple.'"

ELISABETH ELLIOT

"Don't be sorry for yourself because you are going to so
remote a parish. Be sorry for the [Alaskan] Indians.
You know nothing and they must teach you."

MARGARET CRAVEN

In my previous books I have been very careful not to depreciate missionaries unless I was doing it to myself and, God knows, I made my share of mistakes. I resist criticizing others because it causes defensiveness and all the missionaries I know are hard-working and dedicated. I would like to be remembered for my contributions and not my failures, and therefore I should be willing to do the same for others. It is best to take people forward, toward a better alternative, rather than exploiting past negatives. I am now going to break with my tradition and share two stories that reveal a subtle but important point. I would like to think neither of these stories would be true today—but just in case . . .

In 1970 my wife and I attended our first field missionary conference only weeks after arriving in South Africa.[1] Missionaries gathered from the regions to fellowship, worship and strategize together for a week. Two things struck me as a bit peculiar even though at the time I could not really give a name to what I was sensing.

First, the guest speakers were white, usually from a large supporting church in the United States or the home office. From one perspective it was rather pleasant to hear from someone who spoke like me and whom I fully understood. I could relax and soak in the teaching. *But,* I wondered, *where was the voice of the national pastor or Bible teacher?* A logical explanation suggested this conference was only for missionaries. Therefore, nationals would not be present. But in retrospect I think another message also emerged, especially to the nationals: when the missionaries want to learn and grow spiritually, they must bring in one of their own kind. This leads me to the other part of the conference that gave me pause.

I heard a refrain several times during the week: "It is so good to be here. All year we have been giving out, giving out, giving out. Now it is time to take in." At one level I fully appreciated having a speaker from my home country who thought and talked like me. But at another level I found the remark disturbing. It seemed to me that people who said these things were also saying that the local people didn't nurture them, or nurture them as well.

Here's another example. I was riding with a missionary in Guatemala, and we were bouncing our way over the uneven road. I asked him how he keeps learning and growing in this context. Do the local pastors, through their preaching and fellowship, help you grow? The speed with which he answered and the answer itself startled me. Matter of factly, he said the local pastors had nothing to offer him, and except for his own private devotions there was no spiritual feeding available. Then he caught himself and said that he actually did have one source of spiritual growth. Once every two months he got cassette tapes from his home church that provided spiritual food to nourish him.

These illustrations from South Africa and Guatemala suggest that some missionaries don't expect to find spiritual resources in the Christians of their host country. This might be understandable if the church were young with few educated pastors. But in both cases the mission had been in their respective countries for decades, and many local pastors had been through Bible school. I have heard similar stories in several other countries.

THE VIRUS OF THE EDUCATED PERSON
(OR THOSE WHO THINK THEY ARE)

There may be a deeper explanation for these situations. Most missionaries possess a basic college education and many a master's or doctoral degree. While commendable, there is a virus that tends to infect such people, myself included. We might call it the "right answer" virus. It invades our mental software, unobtrusively and quietly but systemically and chronically. It's most evident when we frequently correct others or speak on a topic with such authority and finality that people find little or no room for discussion. Another symptom includes the limited ability to learn from others whom we perceive to be less educated or less spiritual. Thus the more educated we are, the less we are inclined to listen, inquire, probe and be open to learning from those we perceive as less educated.[2]

In the early days of my missionary experience, I found myself in a Bible study led by a layperson who was well meaning but had no formal training in Bible or theology, a big red flag for me. My goal was clear. I immediately questioned his assumptions, corrected his hermeneutics, reminded him of the meaning of the original Greek (and Hebrew if I remembered it), and challenged his understanding of the text. I did this in the interest of truth. I thought I was providing a wonderful service to everyone in the Bible study.

Several things happened over the weeks of the study, which I did not realize and did not wish for. The gracious leader felt rejected by me and found it difficult to conduct the study. The other members stopped contributing because they thought I might embarrass them by correcting them. Besides, if they let me speak first that would save time with "unnecessary" discussion. Without realizing it, I had ruined the Bible study. I had created a disaster. It certainly wasn't my intention, but it took me years to figure out the extent to which this virus had crippled me.

If we aren't aware of how others are perceiving us, we will be unable able to control our message. I thought I was communicating a high respect for the Scripture, a desire for truth and a wish to help all the group members grow in grace. I doubt any of my intentions came through. I suspect what they learned from me was how arrogant and insensitive an educated person can be. Keep in mind, I didn't believe I was obnoxious, demanding or even that controlling. But I fear they felt that I was, and for that I am profoundly sorry. I have often wished I could personally apologize to each one.

While this virus is recognized most quickly among the more educated, I fear that it is more epidemic in Westerners who travel and minister in the less-developed world. We see them with less economic goods, less hygiene, less schooling, less housing, less infrastructure, less spiritual maturity, less knowledge and less "toys." We believe that we can help them. So we set out to tell them how it ought to be done. By that, we mean *how we do it in the West*. This "telling" approach produced some negative side effects early in missions and rarely works at all anywhere today. But the tenacious virus persists, and people see it for what is: pride.

MEDICINE TO MINIMIZE THE VIRUS

No medicines exist to kill most viruses in our body. So it is with pride. It will be with us until we are transformed into the likeness of Christ at the resurrection. Until then, we must think of how to minimize its presence and its effects.

Only one remedy exists for this virus: humility. A humble spirit is central to God's kingdom people, and Jesus modeled it throughout his life (Mt 18:10-14; Lk 14:7-11; Jn 13:4-11). Paul places humility at the heart of serving others (Phil 2:3-5). In *Celebration of Discipline* Richard Foster says, "More than any other single way, the grace of humility is worked into our lives through the Discipline of service."

LEARNING IS . . .

How would you finish this sentence: "Learning is . . ."? If you are like me, it's not an easy assignment. Think about it for a moment. For the purpose of this book, learning is *the ability to glean relevant information about, from and with other people.* Each of the definitions given in this book—*openness, acceptance, trust* and *learning*—began with "the ability." This is intentional. An *ability* is something we can do, do better and even master.

As the definition indicates, I am suggesting three kinds of learning: (1) *about* others, (2) *from* others, and (3) *with* others. We tend to believe that once we have learned *about* someone, we know them. Learning *from* and *with* others is less easily accomplished and doesn't come naturally for many of us. However, serving others is unlikely to happen unless we become somewhat accomplished in all three types of learning.

Learning about. As we consider entering another culture, the natural thing is to begin learning about the people of that culture. This kind of learning is quite well defined for us. We take some classes, read books, check out some issues of National Geographic, watch a film, talk to others who visited or are from that culture, read some "Country Profiles" the government publishes and access Internet Websites. Such sources help us get a basic orientation to the people and their culture.

Learning *about* helps us check and better adjust our expectations against reality. Learning *about* should generate questions that will help us probe more deeply into the culture once we arrive. In fact, it is a good idea to make a list of the issues you want to explore with the local people. Why is this important? My experience suggests that we become rather tongue-tied when we begin relationships with people of other cultures. We end up asking mundane and frivolous questions that are fine early on but which wear thin quickly. A prepared list of questions and issues to probe more deeply will allow you to enter many information-rich conversations. The answers you get will bring a wonderful understanding and appreciation for local realities. You'll be surprised by the depth to which people are willing to share. Learning *about* gives us an initial orientation to a new culture—it's a great place to start.

Learning about a people or a culture usually happens from a distance, before departing for the place of service.[3] We remain in the comfort zone of our home culture while taking in information about another people. This learning often comes from someone or some source within our culture, which means we get a second-hand perspective. It's a great place to begin, but we must be alert to a huge danger and several implications.

The major danger of learning *about* is that we may think, even unconsciously, that now we know the people of the other culture. Our attitude may be: I have learned all about them, so now I know them. Several implications grow from thinking we know others simply from learning *about* them:

- Learning stops. That is, we no longer need to learn *from* them. We can just get on with implementing what is "best for their lives"—graciously, of course.

- We construct answers to all their problems without first learning the issues *from* them and building a response *with* them.

- We don't have to get close to our hosts, even while in their culture. What purpose would it serve? We'd be better off getting on with the task rather than "wasting time" talking with people and sharing their life experiences. Friendship-building becomes unnecessary since we already "know" what they need.

- We turn others into objects. We no longer need to treat them as subjects, as human beings, but merely as those who need our wisdom, presence, answers and resources.

- We create dependent relationships. Others rely on us for goals, direction, resources, nurture and status. Such dependency eventually turns bitter because it daily robs people of their dignity.

- We form stereotypes without ever engaging the culture. If we think we know the other person, we won't be open to new knowledge when learning opportunities come.

While living in southern Africa, many of these dangers invaded my own life and ministry. Usually they were unconscious—until I would get jolted into a stark, undeniable awareness. As long as these dangers stayed at the unconscious level I could move along rather smoothly, but when these ungodly attitudes and behaviors stared me in the face, I had to deal with them. There were always three possible responses: (1) denial: certainly I was not guilty of any dehumanizing ways; (2) rationalizing: circumstances warranted my questionable beliefs and practices; and (3) admitting guilt: my life harbored a subtle "spiritual colonialism" that was fearfully similar to that of the apartheid government I lived in.

Yet important goals can be achieved when we learn *about*. It

- allows us to achieve more accurate expectations when entering another culture

- helps us prepare physically, emotionally, mentally and spiritually for life in a new place so we have more realistic expectations

- should generate questions that we can use to engage the local people over weeks, months and years in our learning *from* mode

- can be done predeparture while information is less threatening in our home culture

- may be all the information you can get if you are on a short-term assignment and time for learning *from* will be limited

- can be done from someone who has bridged both cultures and can communicate information in our native language

Learning too much in the wrong direction. Most of our schooling crams us with content to build our competence in a certain discipline or subject. It prepares us for vocations like church planting, investment banking, medical research and so on. However, in our push for knowledge and technical competency we often overlook the one element that determines success or failure. The Canadian International Development Agency (CIDA) discovered this overlooked element some years ago. They conducted a study that asked, "What characteristics does a person need to be effective overseas?" Before you read further, what do you think are the most powerful factors in overseas effectiveness?

The CIDA study, replicated several times, demonstrated that, far and away, the most powerful factor in overseas effectiveness was the ability to initiate and sustain interpersonal relationships with the local people. Solid, long-term relationships with host country people was the most important contributor to (1) satisfaction in one's overseas assignment, (2) transferring technology to local people, and (3) the ongoing success of the projects (sustainability).

The second major predictor of success was a strong sense of self-identity, which allowed people to be real with each other. People who are comfortable with themselves tend to be authentic and avoid pretense in relationships. We all prefer to deal with "real" people not a façade.

The third major predictor was positive, realistic predeparture expectations.[4] This relates to an individual's ability to anticipate the "bumps" in working in another culture but also to know that life in another culture can be very rewarding. Awareness of our predeparture expectations helps decrease frustration and disappointment. Virtually all our frustrations come when something unexpected happens. What are your emotions when your expectations are violated? Anger? Tension? Revenge? Suspicion? Distrust? Nearly all our responses to unfulfilled expectations are negative. When these negative emotions are expressed to local people whom you feel were in some way responsible, relationships will be strained.

All three characteristics are important. Did you notice one item was missing from the CIDA list? It was technical competency! It ranked fourth in the list, certainly not unimportant, but it was not as statistically significant as the other three. Our ability to do the job (technical competency) was not nearly so important to overseas success as were good interpersonal skills. Think of it this way: interpersonal skills made people successful as they applied their job skills.

As you reflect on your schooling, was the emphasis more on technical or relational competency? Don't get me wrong; knowing how to do your job is important. Often life depends on doing our jobs well. But when it comes to working in another country or with another ethnic group, the research suggests we give priority to building and sustaining relationships.

Learning *about* others—their history, culture, values, religious practices, language, families, organizational structures and other facets of life—is a good place to start. Being good at what we do is also admirable. But the CIDA study shows that learning *about* is insufficient for effectiveness. We can learn *about* without building a single relationship. Therefore, we must pursue more productive kinds of learning.

Learning from. For several reasons learning *from* others is considerably more powerful than learning *about* others. When we learn *from* someone, it is one of the great honors we bestow on them. When we ask questions, seek understanding and probe their thoughts, we are saying, in effect: I need you to teach me. I can't do this alone. I may even fail unless you help me with your knowledge and insights. The act of listening shows respect for the speaker and helps build a sense of community.

Asking others to teach us not only honors them (showing acceptance) but also gives them permission to tell us what they actually see, feel, know and experience. That is, they are less inclined to tell us what they think *we want to hear* and more inclined to tell us what *we need to hear.* There is a huge difference. However, they won't reveal their hearts and honest thoughts unless they first of all trust us.

Getting to know each other as human beings usually (but not always) destroys most stereotypes, prejudice and racism that may lurk within us. When we stop learning at the *about* stage, we "know" people in a distant, impersonal way. They easily become abstract facts like geography or exports. However, learning *from* them affirms them as human beings. They are people who love, hurt, play, dream—like ourselves.

Learning *from* others not only honors them and invites them to speak openly and honestly with us but also establishes interpersonal awareness. Such awareness forms the basis for dialogue. Ruel Howe, author of *The Miracle of Dialogue,* forcefully comments:

> In monologue a person is concerned only for himself and that, in his view, others exist to serve and confirm him. . . .
>
> Dialogue is that address and response between persons in which there is a flow of meaning between them in spite of all the obstacles that normally would block the relationship. It is that interaction between persons in which one of them seeks to give himself as he is to the other, and seeks also to know the other as the other is. . . . At some moment, in the monologue, one participant may give up his pretenses and lay aside the masks by which he seeks the approval and good will of the other, dare to be what he is in relation to the other, invite the other to be a partner in dialogue and be fully present to him as he really is. . . . Any relationship less than this

would not be dialogue and, therefore, not communication. Rather, it would be the exploitation of the other or the ignoring of him or flight from him.[5]

When the "virus" of education infects us, we are prone to monologue—one person dominating the communication. In dialogue two or more people attempt to clarify not only their own thoughts but to explore and understand the thoughts of the other. This is the basis for entering into authentic relationship and the possibility of deep learning *from* each other.

Abusive relationships. People who intend to stay in another culture for several years often enroll in a language school. For one or two years the person learns language *from* the local language teacher. Thus Westerners (or those making the cultural transition) are forced into the learner role.[6] However, most of us see this learner role as temporary, something from which to escape as soon as possible. Once the language has been sufficiently mastered, we again avoid the learner role. I attribute this to our strong sense of independence, our discomfort with interdependence and our focus on getting the task done. We dislike being dependent on others.

Being a learner for only a relatively short period of time, as in learning a language, can appear abusive and utilitarian to the local people. Why? It may appear abusive when the relationship formed with the language teacher is discarded at the end of the course. It appears utilitarian because the relationship is maintained only as long as it has value to the language learner. The teacher is simply the means to an end and may feel used. Transient, utilitarian relations communicate a low view of people.

Dialogue, friendship and solidarity with others require some interdependence. While independence and dependence have serious downsides, interdependence is nothing more than confessing that we need each other for family, church and social well-being.

The real danger. Refusing to be a learner is the real danger. It means that while we are in another culture, we think we know everything necessary to accomplish our task. Interaction with local people is reduced to getting the job done rather than learning more *from* them and becoming increasingly wise in understanding local realities. Instead, our brief exchanges become mutual monologues. We live mostly detached from the local people, periodically reattaching for the pursuit of our goals.

Successful people in overseas ministry value people first. They may not be naturally gregarious, but they work at communicating respect to others. The task at hand then emerges quite easily out of interpersonal connectedness. Effectiveness depends on our willingness to prepare well prior to departure for the new culture (learning *about*) and engaging in learning *from* the people of the culture for language learning and, more importantly, for lifelong learning. We must cultivate the learning role for the duration of our time in the other culture. Such efforts will be well rewarded. Our supervisor, colleagues or financial supporters may push us to get on with the job. I consider this short-sighted. There is no reason why both—relationships and tasks—cannot be done simultaneously.

Getting "new parents." A friend of mine took seriously the learning *from* and learning *with*. Upon entering the new culture he realized he was a "babe" in his understanding. After language school he still felt the need for a cultural partner, someone who could mentor him. He realized that unless someone was willing to help him, he could commit major blunders without even knowing it.

"Dave" looked around for someone he could connect with—a mature and wise local person who would befriend him. After a series of friendly chats with Mr. Yaka, Dave approached him and said something like the following:

> I admire you as a wise and mature person. I realize that I am new
> in your culture and so I am only a baby in my knowledge and understanding. I am in need of help so I can learn about your culture

and the ways of your people. For this I am asking you to be my father, to teach me, to guide me, to protect me. I will be to you a son who promises to learn from you and follow your advice. As my father, you will speak the words I need to hear so I may think and act wisely in your country. As your son, I will listen, obey and grow more wise. Will you be my father and let me be your son?

Mr. Yaka agreed to the relationship. Not only did they become "father" and "son" but eventually partners in taking an effective evangelistic program to many other countries on the continent. They forged a partnership of the soul that bonded them for many years of fruitful ministry.

Sleeping on the floor. Dave was quite well educated; he had a distinguished career as a pilot in the Air Force and was gifted in a way that would have brought him success in any number of ventures. Mr. Yaka had little education and little to suggest that he could mentor Dave. Early on in their relationship, though, something very significant happened.

The two companions had arrived at a place where they were to speak at a conference. The person greeting them said to Mr. Yaka, "I am very sorry but would you be willing to sleep on the floor of this classroom. We have a straw mat and blanket for you." Mr. Yaka graciously agreed. Then the greeter turned to Dave and said, "We have only one bed left, which we have been holding for you. If you come with me I will show you to your room." At this point Dave hesitated only slightly before saying, "Sir, I thank you for being concerned for my comfort. But if you don't mind, I would really prefer staying with my friend, Mr. Yaka. He and I have things to discuss. Would you be so kind as to bring me a mat and blanket?"

How do you think Mr. Yaka felt at this point? What prompted Dave to do this? Was it his need to "discuss things" or was there a deeper reason? In what ways did Dave's decision contribute to the relationship? Would you have taken the bed over the mat on the clay floor? Why or why not? If Dave had taken the bed, what difference might that have made in their relationship? What does Dave's decision tell you about being a servant? About humility?

Sometimes, establishing strong relationships with local people hinges on the kind of attitude we have about ourself and the local people. I'm not sure Dave realized in that split-second decision what a profound message he was sending to his "father," Mr. Yaka, and the long-term impact it would have on them and their ministry—even the continent!

What about you? If you decide you would like to ask some local person to be your guide, teacher, mentor or "father"/"mother," be attentive to whom and how soon you choose. Don't be hasty. Find someone who is respected in the community, and some of that respect will eventually be transferred to you if all goes well. Also be attentive to the motives of your heart. The integrity of your decision will likely be tested on more than one occasion.

I have another friend who chose to work under the local authority in a Bible college. After Ken and his wife had done a good job of learning the language, Ken, well trained and ready to jump into the teaching ministry of the school, found himself doing maintenance work, furniture building and repair, and other menial tasks. That was the assignment given him by the school leader. His wife was given a great job teaching English in the same school. She had the prestigious teaching job; he did manual work. At first Ken grated at this demeaning role, but he pondered the biblical teaching on humility and servanthood and how it ought to speak to his situation: *God knows all about this,* he thought. *He is wise and trustworthy. He doesn't make mistakes. God is God, and I must believe he is present and cares. I am the problem. I have the wrong attitude. I must trust God who is absolutely trustworthy.* Armed with this reaffirmation of who God is, Ken adjusted his behavior accordingly. Equipped with this new perspective, Ken plunged happily into his daily work doing the best job possible without complaint.

About a year later, the president of the school came to Ken and announced that he would like Ken to be his assistant. This was a better position than Ken had ever dreamed about. Soon he was happily engaged in his new role.

Both Dave and Ken teach us important lessons. But keep in mind that God handles us all differently. Dave had many sleeping-on-the-floor situations. Life was not a smooth success story every day. Ken had about twelve months of wondering what God was up to. Walking in mystery while maintaining a strong faith rarely comes easily. But if we are going to be effective in what God gives us to do, we must be willing to walk in the hard places in order to see what fruit God will bring.

Learning with. We have discussed learning *about,* which for the most part is learning about people and culture from a distance. We also have examined learning *from* as a lifelong attitude that honors others. Now we turn our attention to the rarest form of learning: learning *with.* This wonderful form of learning assumes that the best learning happens in relationship, in mutuality, in partnership where neither side is above or beneath.

Proverbs 27:17 may best express this type of learning: "As iron sharpens iron, so one man sharpens another." Respectful interaction between two people benefits both. Each depends on the other. This interdependence produces a kind of life together that regularly mediates Christ, each to the other. Each is, at the same time, teacher and learner, without either person knowing or caring that those roles are being played out. A strong, resilient trust bonds their relationship. This solidarity fosters the deepest sharing, the joy of authenticity and the wonder of mutually discovering the path of God.

Both parties quickly admit that their respective cultures have been affected deeply by sin and that both cultures have redemptive qualities. By learning *from* and *with* each other, we sharpen our vision and practice in ways that could never happen alone. We need each other. Our connected lives (and cultures) make us better people.

Sometimes *synergy* is used to describe this kind of relationship. *Synergy* means "with energy," added or multiplied energy. Have you ever done something with another person and were amazed at what you accomplished? You could never have accomplished it by yourself—even with twice the time. This is synergy. Remember hearing a band or orchestra warming up before the concert? Each member is independently playing notes or chords, creating noise. But when the conductor raises the baton, together they create glorious music. This is synergy.

Synergy is further illustrated by the following, which I got out of a farm journal:

- one horse can pull 6,000 to 7,000 pounds
- two horses can pull about 18,000 pounds
- two horses trained to pull together can pull 25,000 pounds

When synergy happens between two or more people, the result can be amazing, exhilarating, productive and awesome.

The Son of God entered human culture and learned about its bondage to sin and its inability to reconnect with its Creator apart from divine intervention. Unless we too connect deeply with the people of our host culture, we will neither see nor interpret their situation accurately: their pain, their values, their structures, their social limitations, their dreams, their ethos and pathos. Until we can interpret their situation accurately, we will be like the monkey and the fish; our well-meaning help won't fit their reality. The Christ we show them will be more North American than the true Christ, who can naturally address their culture.

WHAT DOES JESUS LOOK LIKE?

For about fourteen years I have taught a week-long course at the Overseas Ministries Study Center in New Haven, Connecticut. The visiting faculty stay in the same room year after year. About the third year I was there, I walked into a familiar room and saw a new painting. It took me a moment to realize it depicted the triumphal entry of Christ into Jerusalem. But this wasn't immediately obvious because it was unlike all the other pictures I had seen of this grand event. Christ was portrayed as thin, dark-skinned, with fine features, a narrow-pointed head covered by black greasy hair punctuated with white daisylike flowers.

The painter was Balinese, and all the people in the painting were Balinese. The Christ figure was on a donkey while others placed the palm leaves in his path and stood in awe. Yet I struggled with identifying this as Christ's triumphal entry because I didn't recognize this portrayal of Christ. I'm actually embarrassed to say that my image of Christ in this event was as a light-skinned person surrounded by similar people—people who looked a lot like me. The more I studied the painting, the more I realized how important it was that a Balinese painter show Christ in Balinese features. He identified Christ as one of them! I had identified Christ with my ethnicity and had no difficulty with that. Why did I have difficulty when someone else portrayed Christ with his or her own ethnicity? Is he not the Christ of every nation, tribe and tongue? Now every time I enter the room, I put my luggage down and study afresh the wonder of this picture and the wonder of this Christ who is all things to all people.

A while back I came across a four-page book called *I Am Green*. On the first page was a brief text about a missionary kid (MK) who grows up in two cultures. On the second page was a big blue circle that represented one culture that the MK experiences—the home culture. On the third page was a yellow circle representing the second culture the MK experiences. MKs find they are neither "blue" nor "yellow." The fourth page states, "I AM GREEN," which is the color created by mixing blue and yellow.

While we tend to make Jesus look like our own culture, the reality is that he is comfortable taking on the color of every culture. We should be comfortable with, and even encourage, that as well.

SUMMARY

Let's summarize the forms of learning important for entering and living in another culture.

- Learning *about* others yields facts that help us adjust our expectations and generate fruitful avenues for deeper learning after entering the culture. The danger: we may stop learning and think that now we know everything necessary for ministry. It also tends to create "we-they" categories.

- Learning *from* others yields understanding that moves us into strong, enduring and trusting relationships resistant to colonialistic attitudes and dependency. The danger: we may tire of learning *from* and move into the telling mode; that is, I have the answers.

- Learning *with* others yields authentic partnerships where each probes deeply the mind and heart of the other, bringing interdependent growth and culturally sensitive ministry. "We-they" categories are replaced with "us" categories. The danger: I can't think of any.

Some wonderful biblical teaching supports our being learners. Cultural stories illustrate how it is done. Read on.

LEARNING
Biblical Foundations for Change

"He who dares to teach must never cease to learn."

AUTHOR UNKNOWN

We seek God's perspective on learning. We have spoken from the social sciences and from the voices of people in the Two-Thirds World. Now we let the Scriptures speak both to affirm and to correct. Two particular doctrines inform our thoughts about learning: common grace and the priesthood of all believers. We will also hear more voices illustrating this principle.

COMMON GRACE

The practical doctrine of common grace was lost to me for many years in spite of considerable exposure to Bible teaching. It's such a rich doctrine that it has caused considerable change in my thinking.

Grace, simply stated, is God's goodness and generosity offered to those who do not deserve it.[1] The Bible speaks about two kinds of grace, both of which come from God. Special grace, also called efficacious grace, refers to God's making salvation available to sinners. In Paul's words: "For it is by grace you have been saved, through faith—and this not from yourselves, it is the gift of God—not by works, so that no one can boast" (Eph 2:8-9). God generously shared his goodness with us by offering us salvation through faith in Christ.

Whereas special grace benefits only those who place their trust in Christ, common grace pertains to the wide variety of ways God benefits all people everywhere.[2] Consider:

- God's Spirit restrains the forces of evil so that some measure of law and order is preserved (2 Thess 2:6-7)

- God provides sunshine and rain for the unjust and the just (Mt 5:45; Acts 14:17)

- God restrains his anger toward evil while being great in loving kindness (Ps 145:8-9)

- God withholds immediate judgment, giving people opportunity to acknowledge their sin and repent (Gen 6:3; Rom 2:4)

- God reveals his "eternal power and divine nature" to all people (Rom 1:20)[3]

In chapter four I mentioned that God has endowed all people with his image. This is part of God's common grace. This means that even unregenerate persons (the unsaved; those not yet in relation with Christ) bear God's image, though warped and distorted by sin. Because they are image-bearers, they are capable of doing good things (e.g., helping others, being kind to their spouse and children, sending money to people stricken by disaster, building orphanages and creating hospitals). These manifestations of common grace ought to remind us of God's own goodness and lead us to trust in him exclusively.

Furthermore, all people can contribute to society, even those who deny Christ. Atheist scientists' discoveries benefit us; non-Christian airplane pilots safely fly us around the globe; unbelieving medical doctors facilitate healing by their understanding of how the human body works. Mechanics, dentists, engineers, farmers, astronauts, store clerks—all are blessed by God even though they don't acknowledge him as Creator.

This is common grace. But what does this have to do with culture, learning and being an effective cross-cultural worker?

COMMON GRACE AND YOU IN A NEW CULTURE

By virtue of being made in the image of God and God's common grace, every person—the atheist, the agnostic, the Hindu, the Muslim, the animist, the outcast, the uneducated, the poor and even our enemy—can contribute to our learning.

Most of us enter another culture, get to know some Christians and find them valuable sources of information, but we often overlook the people in the marketplace, offices, rural villages, hospitals, banks, post offices, taxies and buses. We overlook them as people we can learn *from* and *with* because unconsciously we may see them as having nothing to offer.

We often think, *The Christians of this country can help us, but what can pagans teach us?* So we ignore what could be learned from non-Christians. Later, when we try to witness to them about God's love and Christ's forgiveness, it sounds foreign, very Western. Witness not grounded in the local cultural realities has historically led to the claim that Christianity is a "white man's religion" or "foreigners' religion."

Jesus fits comfortably into all cultures, but we have to learn how to express him in the local context. Only when we show openness toward everyone in the new culture, demonstrate acceptance, build trust and learn from others can we hope to portray a Christ who will look more like the local people than us—more Balinese among the Balinese, more Chinese among the Chinese, more Chilean among the Chileans, and more Zambian among the Zambians. Doing such requires enormous change on our part. Such transformation, such contextualization does not occur naturally. But the effort is worth it. The insights and skills covered in this book move us to learn from all people, an important step in serving them.

One caution: while we can learn from everyone, when there is conflict between cultural truths and the truth found in Scripture, Scriptural truth prevails. Discernment is a necessary skill in gleaning knowledge, whether through creation, other believers or unbelievers. While God reveals his truth through all these sources, our final authority for truth is the Bible. Having said this, we must also be careful not to mistake our own cultural values with biblical truth.

SHANGAAN BIRTHING ATTENDANTS

My wife, Muriel, ranks among the best in gleaning information *from* others in order to serve them effectively. Some years ago she worked for World Relief Corporation, the relief and development arm of the National Association of Evangelicals. Her role as a health specialist gave her responsibility for about a half million children under the age of five who were considered "at risk"—in danger of dying before their fifth birthday. At that time about forty thousand children under five died of a preventable disease every day. In the seven countries she worked in, her job was to provide instruction to the quarter million mothers on how to keep their children alive.

On one trip into southern Mozambique, an African country ravaged by war and poverty, Muriel told her team of local health workers that there was only one purpose in this visit to the villages: to learn *from* the women. That seemed an easy assignment, but Muriel knew from previous experiences the compelling urge that overcomes the experts to jump into conversations, correct misinformation and tell people what they ought to do. The experts then depart feeling they have been successful. (This same urge haunts most Western experts, including short- and long-term missionaries.)

Muriel had arranged for all the Shangaan "grannies" (older women) and birth attendants (those who assisted pregnant mothers in the birthing process because doctors and nurses were unavailable) to gather in the village at a certain time. When they did, Muriel opened the conversation by saying that she and her team of health workers were there to help them be better at assisting the pregnant women in bringing healthy babies into the world and keeping them healthy. "But," my wife said, "you must first help us. We need your help to fight these diseases that are killing your children. Too many of your children are dying at birth or soon after. If we work together we can kill these diseases. Remember, 'it takes two thumbs to squash a louse.' "

Here Muriel used a local proverb to catch the attention of the people and illustrate her point. Lice are hard to kill. You can place them between two fingers and rub, but their small, crusty bodies survive. So to kill a louse, you must put it on a thumb nail and then bring the other thumb nail down on it with pressure. Caught between these two hard surfaces, the louse is killed.

Muriel continued. "You are one thumb, and we health workers are the other thumb. If we work together we can kill the 'lice,' the diseases that are destroying our children." The women nodded in agreement and laughed that this foreign woman should use one of their own proverbs so wisely. As the women relaxed, already feeling some trust, my wife asked the critical questions that would open the door to learning.

She asked, "When the women of your village become pregnant, what advice, what teaching do you give them so they will have healthy children? What do you tell them they should do and should not do?" The women were eager to inform her. None of the experts who had visited their village before seemed interested in learning *from* them. But this woman, Muriel, was different. Common grace says we can learn from anyone. Muriel believed in common grace and the dignity of every person (God's image-bearer). She knew that dignity is a very tender part of each person. It can easily be bruised and, when it is, trust vanishes, sharing stops, learning ceases and serving becomes difficult. The Shangaan women taught my wife and the other health workers for several hours. What they learned became critical to serving that village as the next story attests. It shows how common grace works even in a context where few are Christians but where God is at work.

LEARN FROM THE CHICKEN

The Shangaan grannies and birth attendants had been teaching the pregnant women that they should not eat eggs. Muriel and the other health workers had to control their shock because that would have communicated rejection to the women, and they may have stopped sharing. Calmly, my wife asked the grannies and birth attendants, "This is most interesting. Why do you advise the pregnant women not to eat eggs?"

Again, the women happily answered, somewhat surprised that this foreign "expert" would not have such basic knowledge. The women burst out with the obvious: "You know the chicken, when it wants to lay an egg, it gets all hatchedy, anxiously dances around and appears upset. Well, she is trying to hold the egg back. So if the women eat eggs, they will try to hold the baby back, keep it from being born, causing difficulty in the childbirth. So they must not eat eggs when they are pregnant."

This tidbit of knowledge was a wealth of information for Muriel. It explained the high incidence of childhood eye disease, including early blindness and poor nutrition during pregnancy. The yolk of the egg contains a high concentration of vitamin A, necessary for normal eye development. But a sticky problem remained.

Since the health workers were committed only to learning, not to giving corrective information during this session, they registered the data and determined to return to this problem later in the new health lessons. It was very difficult to keep from shouting out the right answer to the problem: "They need eggs for healthy development of their babies' eyes. Don't give them that bad advice!" At the end of the session, when all the questions had been asked and all the information volunteered, Muriel thanked the grannies and birth attendants for their wonderful help. She further noted that they were truly remarkable people for their dedication to the mothers and the well-being of the entire village. Many healthy children and adults in the village were testimony to their efforts.

Were these grannies and birth attendants perfect in their advice to the pregnant mothers? Of course not. But they were doing the best they could with the insight they had. And over the years they had accumulated considerable wisdom that provided the village with the degree of health it did have. But the sticky problem was yet unresolved: how to correct misinformation.

Build face, save face, but don't lose face. Muriel's awareness of cultural values had grown during her childhood years as a missionary kid growing up in rural Zimbabwe. She knew the importance of not causing people to lose face, that is, to feel shame, humiliation and disgrace, especially among their peers.[4] Therefore, at the end of their conversation she was lavish in her praise of these women for their efforts. That is called "building face" or making them look good, affirming them, heralding their virtues. She ended the meeting by thanking the women and expressing admiration for all the hard work they do and for the wisdom they shared.

The health messages about vitamin A were later woven into the stories used in the health curriculum for that village. Featured in these stories were pregnant women who were encouraged to eat generous amounts of food sources containing vitamin A. As for the admonition not to eat eggs, that too was woven into a story very carefully. Over time, the message that the egg was good and the yellow yolk was very important in preventing eye diseases in infants was accepted by the village because they trusted the health workers.

All the health messages were eventually accepted, but we must look at the context that made their acceptance possible. First, Muriel called together all the "experts" who assisted in instructing pregnant women and assisted in the birthing process. Then she generously complimented them. She used a local proverb. She showed no disdain or rejection at anything they said. Then she and the other health workers used the story method of teaching. Stories are among the most effective tools for teaching people information. Think of the openness, acceptance, trust and learning that Muriel demonstrated. In this kind of context she was able to serve the Shangaan women and the entire village.

Note that Muriel did not call the young women, married women or pregnant women of the village together and announce that they should all eat eggs to prevent eye disease in their unborn children. To do so would have brought enormous shame and loss of face to the grannies and birth attendants. They would have looked foolish and lost all respect from the other villagers. My wife, of course, would have gained enormous respect and admiration for bringing such important information. But that was not her mission. Her mission was to serve the Shangaan people, not by embarrassing them but by making their grannies and birth attendants wiser and better able to make good decisions. Nor did she even call this group together to tell them they were wrong about the eggs. She never corrected them directly on that point. To do so would have caused them to lose face and feel guilty whenever they saw a blind child in the village. As a result of her careful efforts, the Shangaan women called Muriel "our Mother."

Serving people is not just doing what seems good in *our* own culture but seeking out the knowledge of the people, learning from them, knowing their cultural values and then acting in ways that support the fabric of the culture to the degree possible. After taking these steps, we will have served them.

Rice water. Muriel also worked in Cambodia. Health experts there discovered that Khmer mothers fed rice water (a cereal-based fluid) to their children when they had diarrhea (once the leading cause of death among children under five). About the same time, international medical experts, to their surprise, discovered that the nutrients of the cereal-based fluids proved the most effective way to treat diarrhea, keeping the children hydrated and providing necessary nutrients. The Khmer mothers had discovered some of God's wisdom—God's common grace revealed to preliterate people—which eventually the Western experts also discovered. They have learned something about how God structures his world and, while they don't acknowledge him, thank or honor him for his kindness, he graciously gives them this knowledge. In so doing, he shows his care for them and their children. He also reveals his own character though they may choose not to recognize it. Learning *from* them—what they have discovered about God's ways—helps us be better servants.

God Blesses the Farmer

Consider how God (through Isaiah) illustrates his common grace in the life of the farmer:

> Listen and hear my voice;
>> pay attention and hear what I say.
> When a farmer plows for planting, does he plow continually?
>> Does he keep on breaking up and harrowing the soil?
> When he has leveled the surface,
>> does he not sow caraway and scatter cummin?
> Does he not plant wheat in its place,
>> barley in its plot,
> and spelt in its field?
> *His God instructs him*
>> *and teaches him the right way.*
> Caraway is not threshed with a sledge,
>> nor is a cartwheel rolled over cummin;
> caraway is beaten out with a rod,
>> and cummin with a stick.
> Grain must be ground to make bread;

so one does not go on threshing it forever.
Though he drive the wheels of his threshing cart over it,
   his horses do not grind it.
All this comes from the LORD *Almighty,*
   wonderful in counsel and magnificent in wisdom.
(Isaiah 28:23-29, italics added)

Isaiah takes us to a scene that his contemporaries could visualize.
They had seen it hundreds of times. But Isaiah forces the reader to think
about God through the farmer's routine. The farmer plows his field but
does not keep on plowing over and over. Why not? How does he know
when the field is ready? How does he know what to do next and when
to do it? Where does this wisdom come from?

God generously shares his knowledge and wisdom with those he has
created. The problem comes when his creatures refuse to recognize him
as the source of their knowledge and fail to thank him for it. Then, as
Paul says:

> For although they knew God, they neither glorified him as God
> nor gave thanks to him, but their thinking became futile and their
> foolish hearts were darkened. Although they claimed to be wise,
> they became fools and exchanged the glory of the immortal God
> for images made to look like mortal man and birds and animals
> and reptiles. (Rom 1:21-23)

Even though truth is suppressed by non-Christians, they still bear the
image of their Creator and are recipients of his common grace; thus they
are able to know and communicate the things God has revealed to them.
This was my experience at Michigan State University, where most professors did not acknowledge the God who is "magnificent in wisdom."
But I was pleasantly surprised by many of my professors who, while giving no evidence of a God consciousness, were disciplined in the pursuit

of truth. I found that many insights from the social sciences were consistent with Scripture or, at worst, did not contradict Scripture. Common grace means we must be learning *about, from* and *with* others, regardless of where they fall on the faith spectrum, be they village grannies or the intellectual elite.

The doctrine of common grace instructs us to glean truth from every source in God's world.

PRIESTS: YOU AND ME

First Peter 2:5 declares all believers "a holy priesthood." All members of the church, worldwide, are priests. This truth has two beautiful dimensions: vertical and horizontal. The vertical dimension relates to the fact that as New Testament priests we can now approach God through Christ anytime, anywhere and under any conditions. No travel to a designated place, no waiting, no intermediary. God is directly accessible to us at any moment (Heb 4:14-16; see also Rom 5:1-5; 1 Tim 2:5). In the Old Testament, priests came only from the tribe of Levi. When people wanted access to God they had to do so at specified times, a specified place and with a specified offering (Lev 1—7). Now with Christ as our great high priest we have no limitations on connecting with our heavenly Father.

Priest to priest. Old Testament priests also had a horizontal dimension. Not only did they represent the people before God, usually through temple offerings and sacrifices, but they daily mediated God and his grace to the other eleven tribes—a horizontal function. By mediate, I mean that they communicated the mind and purposes of God to the other Israelites as best they could. In doing so, they were communicating God's grace to the people. As New Testament believers we too have a similar horizontal function—to share our understanding of God and his purposes to each another. This teaching is implicit throughout the New Testament but is explicit in passages that talk about the connectedness of the body of Christ and the interdependence of the parts of the body.[5]

This truth has profound implications for how we relate to each other in virtually every sphere of life.

Underage priests? The horizontal dimension of the priesthood of all believers struck me when my oldest son, Scott, at about age seven, placed his trust in Christ as his Savior. The thought struck me that now he is a priest. What does that mean? It means two things: as a member of the body of Christ he now has access to his heavenly Father through Jesus Christ any time, any place and under any circumstances. He is connected to God in a new wonderful way. That pleased me and brought me significant comfort. I struggled more with the second part: as a New Testament priest he was now able to mediate Christ to other believers, including me! At seven years of age? To me, a Bible school and seminary graduate? I had to ponder this implication.

It was true. Not only was Scott now connected to God in a new way but he also was connected to me and others in a new way. As a priest he could mediate Christ to me and others. Would he do it with much wisdom? Probably not. With much sophistication? Probably not. With much knowledge of the Scripture? Certainly not at age seven. The implications were not terribly staggering for my son, but they were for me. I must acknowledge his priesthood and treat him as a priest. Meaning what? Now I had to remind myself that Christ is his Lord, the Holy Spirit dwells within him, he is gifted by God, and I must attend to his words, ideas, thoughts and perceptions because at any time God may speak to me through my young son.

I can't dismiss his voice on a matter because it could well be the voice of the Lord. I couldn't discard his position as we brought family matters to the table for discussion. His position may be God's direction. I couldn't ignore his thoughts on Scripture since his youthful eyes may, in fact, be seeing what God wants me to see. I always had to be alert to the possibility that God's own voice may be in the voice of my son.

The global priesthood of brothers and sisters. Now let's take this truth into the cross-cultural context. God has his followers planted everywhere, sometimes liberally and sometimes sparingly. But wherever we encounter them, they are part of his holy priesthood. They are as able as any of us to mediate his marvelous grace—if we are able to receive it. If we suppose ourselves to be more educated, we may think that we have come to give God's grace and wisdom to them and that they have little to offer us in return. Remember the missionary in Guatemala who said he could get no spiritual nurture from the local pastors? He was ignoring the priesthood of all believers. He was putting himself over them in such a way that all the nurturing was one way, from him to them. But for the priesthood of all believers to function properly, we must all nurture each other, listen to each other, see the beauty of Christ in each other and seek God's grace from each other.

It is very easy, especially when we are entering a rather economically poor part of the world, to believe (probably unconsciously) that we are called to spiritually feed people, educate them in the Bible and show them how to live the holy life. I know I slip into this unbiblical posture too often and find myself doing the "Pharisee" thing: looking down on others, taking a master role, and lording it over them with my knowledge, titles and degrees (see Mt 20:25-28; 23:5-12). Like the disciples I prefer wearing the robe of privilege rather than picking up the towel of service (see chapter 2). In my more sane moments, and I hope they are increasing, I attempt to see other believers, wherever I meet them, as Jesus told us to see them: "You have only one Master and you are all brothers" (Mt 23:8).

The designation "brothers" puts us all on the same plane; notice we are not categorized as elder or younger brothers—just brothers, with Christ as our Master. This metaphor of brotherhood ties us together as distinct but equals. Brotherhood and sisterhood connects us interdependently, each playing an important role but also needing each other in order for the family to function. The idea of priesthood suggests that each of us is able to minister the grace of God to anyone else and be ministered to by anyone else. Thus we are both teachers of and learners with each other. All three images clearly identify Christ as the unifying master of the family, head of the body, and high priest of the temple. These three important roles function most effectively when Christ's proper position is recognized and we stay in our positions as brothers and sisters loving one another, body members dependent on each other, and priests mediating Christ to one another. Sometimes, though, people have difficulty seeing themselves in a priestly role.

I'm just a farmer. While we were on furlough from our ministry in South Africa, a small Wisconsin church needed a pastor, and I needed some income. So I became the interim pastor. I brought an issue to the church board for discussion. As I probed their minds for insight, one fellow, a farmer, spoke up and said, "Pastor, you have all the training. You've studied Greek and Hebrew and theology. You know the Scriptures. You should be telling us what we should do. I'm just a farmer." I know he was paying me a compliment, but his statement also indicated that he didn't think he had any wisdom to offer when someone more educated was in the room. I told him that the people of God elected him to this office because they believed that he met the biblical requirements. Thus he represented a part of the wisdom of God that should be included in the business of the church. He had difficulty wrapping his mind around this thought.

I believe that part of the problem is historical. Former pastors of the church, whom I knew to some degree, had a different approach to leadership. They operated as the decision-makers, using the board as a "sounding board" for their ideas. Thus the church's lay leaders were used to being the pastors' "rubber stamps." I'm convinced many of us from the West have unwittingly done the same to church leaders in the other countries. We have overlooked their priestly function. Instead, we give the right answers, make the decision and "share" the vision God has for this ministry. I believe that our failure to recognize and practice the priesthood of all believers has led to major flaws in the understanding and practice of Christian leadership in the global church. By developing and practicing a few skills, we can restore the priestly function of all believers.

SKILLS

Paul Goring, a thirty-year missionary veteran from Colombia, South America, offers some insights. He researched personality characteristics of missionaries and their effect on communication with others.[6] Among his conclusions was this:

> In broad terms, the people who can be categorized as duty-bound and anxious to conserve resources are twice as numerous among the missionary population as among the U.S. population. This type of person—as a missionary—is interested in transmitting communication more than in receiving it. Missionaries with this personality are anxious that their extremely important message be heard. . . . They are the ones who can get things done! However, they also tend to be less sensitive, less likely to understand the situation of their hearers, and less concerned about integrating into the host culture.

What struck you from this paragraph? Read it again.

Dr. Goring found that 76 percent of the missionaries—twice the percentage found in the U.S. population—fell into the "duty-bound" category and were more "interested in transmitting communication . . . than in receiving it." These people are wonderfully motivated for the task but are less effective because they lack certain skills.

Listening. William Stringfellow said, "Listening is a rare happening among human beings."[7] Do you agree? Reflect on your own relationships. How would you rate yourself as a listener? Do you have a friend or acquaintance who is a good listener? How does he or she make you feel? Stringfellow went on to say:

> You cannot listen to the word another is speaking if you are preoccupied with your appearance or with impressing the other, or are trying to decide what you are going to say when the other stops talking, or are debating about whether what is being said is true or relevant or agreeable. Such matters have their place, but only after listening to the word as the word is being uttered.

Look again at the list of hindrances Stringfellow gives. Which most interferes with your ability to listen? Can you name other things that distract you when you should be listening attentively?

Listening may be one of the most effective expressions of love for this reason: it honors the person speaking. It also communicates that you are willing to be taught by the one speaking. In being good listeners we allow the other person to have access to our mind and heart. In so doing we become vulnerable to the other person. This isn't a negative thing if we exercise some discernment. In fact, it can be profoundly positive because listening often gives us access to the voice of God through one of his servants.

> **"Listening is a primitive act of love."**
>
> WILLIAM STRINGFELLOW

Another reason for listening carefully, especially in another cultural context, is that people respond to a good listener by sharing more deeply and intimately about themselves. Such was the case with my wife among the Shangaan women in southern Mozambique. One health worker who had been working among the Shangaan for twenty years told Muriel that in all her time there she had never been able to get such important information from them. Muriel learned *from* them by listening to them before she began to teach. People share out of the depths of their lives to those they trust and are good listeners.

Responding. Responding wisely is another skill in the good-listening process. Most of us respond to conversations in rather predictable ways. Psychologist Carl Rogers said there were five ways of responding to people in conversation.[8] His research revealed that the most frequent response North Americans have in conversation is the evaluative response. That is, our responses are characterized by agreeing or disagreeing, by correcting any error we might detect, by giving a counterpoint, by saying "Yes, but . . . ," by changing the subject or by withdrawing. An evaluative response tends to either shift the conversation into debate or closes it down. But we can promote dialogue if we develop one or more of the other responding skills—probing, interpretation, support or understanding. These contribute to a better communication and true dialogue.

We have a choice in how we respond to every encounter with another person. Usually this choice is made unconsciously because we fall into familiar patterns. If the pattern is an evaluative response, there is a good chance that cross-cultural ministry will be minimally effective. Thus we must practice more open responses, such as probing (asking questions that go deeper into the topic), interpretation (saying back in our own words what we've heard the other person say), support (best when feelings are being expressed and empathy is most appropriate), and understanding (asking for more clarification, illustration or detail).

Dialogue. Dialogue contributes to better communication and results in longer and stronger relationships. Good dialogue requires an atmosphere of trust, where people feel accepted and thus can be open about their opinions and beliefs. Dialogue assumes a willingness to learn from the other, thus one's own perspectives and positions are held tentatively. Each person listens carefully and nonjudgmentally to the other and responds in probing, nondefensive ways. Dialogue promotes truthful sharing without manipulative motives. Each must be committed to the best interests of the other without compromising his or her own deeply held principles.

Even in dialogue, it's possible that the parties will not reach an agreement or solve a problem. But it assures all involved that relational stress will be minimal, mutual respect will be preserved and the dignity of each person will not be compromised. Especially when discussing cultural differences, dialogue allows us to hear clearly, to teach and be taught, to find wisdom and even healing in nondefensive communication, and to inspire one another toward faithful servanthood.

SUMMARY

Learning *from* and *with* are not simply good strategies, they are resident in Scripture and touch every part of our relational lives. Common grace tells us we can learn from believers as well as those who do not believe in Christ. We learn *from* and *with* because such activity honors the God who made us brothers and sisters, priests and members of the same body. God in his wisdom placed us together in healthy interdependence so that we will best reflect his glory and accomplish his work. Gladis DePree beautifully summarizes the missionary experience by saying, "Relationships . . . became an integral part of discovering God."[9]

UNDERSTANDING
Seeing Through the Other's Eyes

*"The key for successful personal relationships and ministry
is to understand and accept others as having
a viewpoint as worthy of consideration as our own."*

SHERWOOD G. LINGENFELTER AND MARVIN K. MAYERS

*"No matter how adept an exegete a theologian is, . . . it is
all for naught if he does not understand his contemporary audience."*

MARK E. VAN HOUTEN

In this chapter we start to see how all the material covered previously begins to come together—like the picture of a puzzle when sufficient pieces are in place. This chapter also introduces the idea of perspectivism, seeing as others see. Perspectivism, lacking in much mission literature, is wonderfully embedded in Scripture and is so important for doing God's work.

DEFINITION OF UNDERSTANDING

Understanding is *the ability to see patterns of behavior and values that reveal the integrity of a people.* Let me say it another way: understanding another culture is the ability to see how the pieces of the cultural puzzle fit together and make sense to them and you. Life in another culture is frustrating at first because we do not see the bigger picture, but the wonder of eventually seeing the pieces fit and the picture of understanding appear is exhilarating.

My basic assumption in this chapter is that people usually don't act randomly or stupidly. Those from other cultures may think it random or stupid, but from the local people's perspective, they're thinking or acting out of a larger framework that makes sense to them. People's behavior generally fits within a cultural pattern that works for them and gives them meaning and control in their lives. Too often we assume others are foolish or illogical simply because their reasoning is not self-evident to us.

When we explore the deeply embedded reasons why someone did something, a rational explanation that makes sense to those who share that culture usually emerges. But to those outside of that culture, it doesn't make sense. It's hard to understand why people do what they do. Until we understand, it will be difficult to effectively communicate or to develop any meaningful relationships.

Our visit in Kenya is illustrative. As the Maasai elder approached us, our youngest son, Marc, did as he had been told: "Step forward and bow your head. The elder will put his hand on your head and offer a greeting." It was the way for Maasai children, and we would honor their ways. The Maasai elder proceeded to spit on his head three times. Confusion flooded our minds trying to understand what had just happened. Then Marc stepped back to the side of his mother and said, "Mom, that man spit on me. He spit on me." His mother answered, "Yes, we must wait and see what it means," and the elder stepped forward to greet us in a more traditional Western way.

Later we asked a friend who knew the Maasai how we should interpret the spitting on our son. He laughed and said, "It was a blessing. They do it all the time." Marc didn't feel blessed, and we were skeptical. But with further information we began to understand. The Maasai believe that when it rains on their arid land, God is spitting—God is blessing them. This has a parallel in Scripture, which talks about two kinds of spitting. One was to shame a person by spitting in his or her face (Num 12:14; Deut 25:9; Is 50:6; Mt 26:67). The other kind of spitting was used to bless another person. Different Greek words were used for "spit" meant to shame or bless. Blessing is clearly in mind when Jesus used his spittle in healing people (Mk 7:33; 8:23; cf. Jn 9:6). Our new understanding put everything in perspective.

Maasai also spit in their hands before the handshake to seal a business deal; they spit on infants when they are first brought out into public; and the women rub spit into the forearms of the person they are pleased to see.

A puzzle. A jigsaw puzzle might help us visualize this idea of understanding. As we dump the pieces out on a table, it's a jumbled mass of disconnected pieces. Assume you don't have the front of the box to give you the final picture. Makes things harder, huh? It often feels that way when entering a new culture. All the pieces are there, but they make no sense, and we have no picture to guide us. It's rather daunting.

Assembling the pieces of a culture so we can see the bigger picture and to understand how it all fits together takes patience and perseverance. The transition from seeing a heap of unrelated pieces to seeing the integrated beauty of the culture is a very rewarding journey. Yes, there are parts of any culture that aren't beautiful, just as there are flaws in our own culture, but the "picture" that emerges, piece by piece, should make more and more sense. Just as my family gained insight into the spitting of the Maasai elder, our understanding of any culture comes piece by piece. Each new insight provides ability to function more comfortably and more effectively.

A tapestry. A tapestry also illustrates the process of understanding another culture. A tapestry is pieces of cord or yarn that are woven together to form a picture or design, which when finished is hung on a wall. When we look at the front side of the tapestry, we see the picture. But when we look at the back side of the tapestry, we see a confusion of dangling threads, no pattern or theme. Entering a new culture is like seeing the back side of a tapestry—there's no obvious pattern or picture to help us understand the culture.

We must discipline ourselves to see the patterns of the new culture. Cultural understanding emerges slowly, over time. Occasionally we get a peek at the front side of the tapestry, where bits of pattern emerge. Eventually we are no longer overwhelmed by of the back of the tapestry because we see more and more the pattern on the front. Most of us want this to happen quickly. Actually, it takes months and years to see clearly, because cultures are complex and varied. Nevertheless, we must continually work at it even if our stay is short.

Listen to some experts. Anthropologists Sherwood Lingenfelter and Marvin Mayers comment, "Missionaries, by the nature of their task, must become personally immersed with peoples who are very different. To follow the example of Christ, that of incarnation, means undergoing drastic personal reorientation."[1] The responsibility to change is ours. William Gudykunst, a cross-cultural researcher, says, "One of the major factors influencing our effectiveness in communicating with people from other cultures is our ability to understand their culture."[2] Cornelius Osgood, an expert on China, writes, "The greater the understanding of the people of one society by another, the greater the possibility for meaningful communication, beneficial exchange, increased appreciation and the reduction of fear."[3] Veteran missiologist David Hesselgrave says, "Missionaries must come to an even greater realization of the importance of culture in communicating Christ. In the final analysis, they can effectively communicate to the peo-

> *"Understanding is the basis of care. What you would take care of you must first understand, whether it be a petunia or a nation."*
>
> DALLAS WILLARD

ple of any given culture to the extent that they understand that culture."[4]

Just about any book you read in cross-cultural ministry or cross-cultural communication will emphasize the need for understanding the other person, the other generation, the other ethnic group before attempting any serious communication. Learning a language is an important first step. But learning how to form the message so that it is received by the hearer requires much more commitment to culture learning. Otherwise, we may be nothing more than grammatically correct fools or, as Paul puts it in 1 Corinthians 13:1, "clanging cymbals."

BIBLICAL PERSPECTIVES ON UNDERSTANDING

The Bible exhorts us to understand God and his ways. For example, Job declares that God is so great he is beyond understanding (Job 36:26). Yet he graciously gives understanding of many things (Job 32:8; 1 Jn 5:20). The book of Proverbs tells us to apply our hearts to understanding (Prov 2:2) while being careful not to rely on our own understanding (Prov 3:5). Rather, get your understanding through a "knowledge of the Holy One" (Prov 9:10). Understanding God is priceless (Prov 4:7; 16:16); it's a fountain of life (Prov 16:22). With God as the source of understanding, the wise person will meditate on his Word and contemplate creation, which whispers and shouts the glory of God.

The Bible says we can gain understanding from the general revelation of creation and the special revelation of God's Word. Psalm 19 represents the clearest portrayal of understanding from creation. King David, the writer, exuberantly states that the heavens declare, the skies proclaim, the days speak, the nights reveal, every nook and cranny of creation instructs us. Listen:

> The heavens declare the glory of God;
>> the skies proclaim the work of his hands.
> Day after day they pour forth speech;

night after night they display knowledge.
There is no speech or language
   where their voice is not heard.
Their voice goes out into all the earth,
   their words to the ends of the world. (Ps 19:1-4)

Then David slides seamlessly from the understanding we glean from creation to the understanding we glean from the "law of the Lord" (Ps 19:7). He declares that creation and God's Word are both valuable sources of truth. Creation and Scripture proclaim the same message, because the God, who is the source of all truth, has given us both.

Another passage of Scripture with compelling insight on creation and understanding comes from Paul's letter to the Romans. This passage, harsh in its message, also motivates us to share the good news of forgiveness through Christ's death and resurrection. God's anger is poured out against all humanity because of sin. All humans are guilty and condemned for one reason: we have rejected the understanding of God that comes through creation.

Since what may be known about God is plain to them, because God has made it plain to them. For since the creation of the world God's invisible qualities—his eternal power and divine nature—have been clearly seen, being understood from what has been made, so that men are without excuse.

For although they knew God, they neither glorified him as God, nor gave thanks to him, but their thinking became futile and their foolish hearts were darkened. (Rom 1:19-21)

God speaks through creation and through his Word. People have a choice when God's voice comes to them. Most choose to ignore it. But as long as they draw breath, they may yet respond to his voice—perhaps God's voice through you.

Understanding is important for the following reasons:

• God says that truth is available through the Scripture (special revelation) and through creation (general revelation). By inference, that means we may learn about God as we learn about other cultures. He has not revealed all of his knowledge and wisdom to the Western cultures alone or to any one culture. But each culture can make a significant contribution to our understanding about who God is and how he works in this world.

• When we seek to understand and learn from other cultures, we honor God. God gives us additional insight and wisdom as we gain knowledge from others. Learning and understanding are sacred activities because they draw us closer to God and creation.

• As we understand a new culture, we can more completely fit into it. In earlier days this was called "identification" but is now called "incarnation." *Incarnation* is the theological word for the truth that the Son of God took human flesh, entered human culture and lived as we live (but without sin). Similarly, missionaries are called to incarnate Christ in a new culture by understanding and adjusting to local realities and living out God's kingdom values.

• Understanding brings new perspectives. Assuming we are *open* and have built *trust*, people will share their lives with us. We can learn *from* them and gradually understand the new culture; we acquire new perspectives. The ability to add new perspectives to those we already bring from our own culture is one of the neglected pieces in cross-cultural effectiveness.[5] But there are barriers.

EGOCENTRISM

Egocentrism is *the tendency for each of us to believe that the way we think, believe and act is the best way*—the superior way. We then measure all others by how close they come to "our way." If they are close to our way of thinking and doing things, we accept them, draw closer to them and think positively about them. If they don't "measure up," we become suspicious and try to change them. If they don't respond favorably, we may reject them by avoiding them. There are many ways of showing disfavor. Another word for "measuring" others is to *judge* them. The highly egocentric person regularly evaluates people to see if they live up to his or her standards. If not, they are deemed defective and untrustworthy. But if they measure up, they are received into a circle of trusted friends.

Continuous evaluation of others, usually unconscious, has disastrous effects in cross-cultural friendships. In a new culture nearly everything is different. The tendency then is to judge everything as inferior, needing change, substandard. Our behavior will reveal these underlying attitudes and be seen by local people as judgmental, arrogant, paternalistic—neocolonialistic.

When a group shares common values and wholeheartedly adheres to these, it is called ethnocentrism—a group centeredness—which can be a second barrier to cross-cultural understanding.[6]

ETHNOCENTRISM (REVISITED)

Ethnocentrism—literally ethnic-centeredness or culture-centeredness—is not necessarily bad; after all, we all have group loyalty, even national loyalty. However, it becomes a negative when we are imprisoned by it and resist changing. Carley Dodd explains that ethnocentrism is "the cultural attitude that one's culture or group is superior to another person's culture or group."[7] W. G. Sumner adds another dimension: "Ethnocentrism is the technical name for the view in which one's own group is the center of everything and all others are scaled and rated with reference to it."[8] In egocentrism *my* ways are superior to yours; in ethnocentrism, *our* ways are superior to *yours*. The group believes it is superior. Again, all of us are ethnocentric to some degree. Ethnocentrism is valuable when it creates solidarity among group members and fosters group pride. I have yet to meet anyone not essentially proud of their culture, even if they are among the most poor and marginalized. So if they detect that we look down on their culture, they are naturally hurt. Because most of our egocentrism and ethnocentrism is unconscious, others see it but we are mostly unaware.

Gladis DePree, a missionary to Hong Kong, exposed her ethnocentric attitude when she confessed, "I can't see why people get so perturbed about identifying with the culture. To me, the whole thing is ridiculous. Why shouldn't I be myself? We have our ways and they have theirs."[9] I suspect many of us have mumbled something similar as we struggled to adjust to a new culture. This ugly side of ethnocentrism appears as cultural arrogance. Monitor your thoughts and even your words; see if this is not true. It was true for me more times than I want to believe. Ethnocentrism forever lurks within me, within us! Fortunately, most of us realize it is an unhealthy attitude. So what do we do about it?

STOP COMPARING

I am a firm believer in being aware of my thoughts, fleeting as they may be, and how they influence me. I work at this because I want to jettison some unproductive patterns. For example, even though my South Africa experience was wonderful, in the early days I constantly compared things there with things back home—roads, sanitation, dress, punctuality, living conditions, workmanship, food, driving patterns, smells, church services, leadership styles, decision making, conflict management, relationships, recreation, phone service, organization and so on—until I was exhausted from dealing with all the inferiorities around me, wondering why I ever left home. South Africa, beautiful in so many ways, always came up short. But what good did this comparing do? It didn't change anything and only left me feeling depressed and lonely.

Here is what I did—self-talk. *Stop it!* I told myself maybe twenty or more times a day, *and get on with living here and fitting in.* I had to intentionally interrupt the pattern of judging the new culture. *Stay open. Accept things as they are,* I kept saying to myself. *Remember openness and acceptance! Focus on building trust. Learn. Understand. You can do this.*

In time I broke the negative pattern; I stopped evaluating and criticizing the pieces of the puzzle, and I began to see how they fit together and made sense. Sometimes I slipped, but mostly I began to see people as God's image-bearers with all the dignity he bestowed on them. I saw culture as a puzzle that, seen as a whole, would have striking beauty and integrity. There were obvious scars revealing that sin had its corrupting effect on the culture, but the beauty persisted. I watched others who were adept at navigating the culture to see what attitudes and skills contributed to their understanding. These simple but strategic activities reoriented me in the right direction. And now, thirty-five years later, those skills continue to guide me.

Some comparison is perfectly normal. We often connect a new experience to something in our past. That's OK—for a while. But work on minimizing so you can appreciate the new culture for its own sake, not in reference to your home culture.

LOOK FOR GOOD, BEAUTY AND COMMON GRACE

The Pianist, a movie, recounts the human and physical devastation of World War II. An accomplished Jewish pianist emerges from the rubble of the Warsaw buildings and hides from the occupying Nazis. In the rubble he discovers a piano, and when he is sure no one will hear, he begins to play. In the sound of his own music he finds comfort and temporary escape from fear and gnawing hunger. Soon a German officer who has established an office among the destroyed buildings hears the beautiful music, which also brings momentary peace to his own soul. The officer discovers that the pianist is a Jew. One day the pianist, always on the brink of starvation, sees a package that had not been there the day before. Inside the package is bread. He would live another day. He would play the piano one more time. The bread begins to appear regularly. Both the German officer and the Jewish pianist live by the kindness of the other and, ultimately, by the kindness of God.

The film, dark in nature because of the devastation of war, had rays of good, of beauty, of God's grace: a piano in working condition, music that soothed the hunter and hunted, bread to eat, peace periodically invading the guilty and fearful, and life, raw life. By God's grace people can be kind to each other, create beauty, love each other, build families and cultures. Sin and its effects are always with us, but if we obsess over them we overlook the wonder of God's presence in people and their various cultures. Look for the good and the beautiful, and when you see it you will see God's grace.

CHILDREN MINISTERING GOD'S GRACE

In Rwanda, shortly after the human carnage and while mass graves were still being dug up, my wife and I visited an orphanage in the southern part of the country. Many of the five-to-twelve-year-old children had fled into the jungle during the war. They never found their parents and ended up at this orphanage, which is surrounded by heavy jungle. The buildings were basic. The dorm was one rectangular room with rows of bunk beds only inches apart. Two to four children, depending on size, slept in each bed. They either slept sideways or bigger children would sleep with heads at opposite ends, each dodging the other's feet. There were no toys or balls or playground equipment. Knotted rags served as a soccer ball. Everything was dirt or mud when it rained. Food was minimal.

After the director, an American missionary, showed us around, he called a group of children together and asked them to sing and dance for the unexpected guests. They did, with joyful enthusiasm and infectious smiles. These children, who had nothing but their lives and some rags that passed as clothes, ministered joy to my own heart—and with conviction. So often I complain at small things, momentarily forgetting my incredible wealth in Christ, in my family, in my culture and in my possessions. The orphans, so young with so little, showed me how to see, how to value, how to live and how to recognize God's grace.

PERSPECTIVISM

Another fruitful way to deal with ethnocentrism is getting to know well two or three local people. Doing so should (1) break down any stereotypes and prejudices you may be carrying, (2) give you opportunities to get specific answers to questions, (3) create some positive emotional bonds with host people, (4) provide you with daily companions who can share life's situations with you, and (5) help you get an insider's perspective, that is, help you see things, understand things and interpret the world more as they do.

Getting the insiders' perspective, sometimes called perspectivism or perspective taking, means you begin to see as the local people see.[10] It's like having double vision: seeing the world through your own cultural lenses and also being able to see more and more clearly through the lenses of another culture. Taking another's perspective is never easy; it means we must set aside our ethnocentrism to try to see how they see, to think like they think, to value as they value. This doesn't mean that we set aside any of our biblical principles, just that we get a deeper understanding of the people and culture.

> "It may be difficult to teach a person to respect another unless we can help people to see things from the other's point of view."
>
> KOHEI GOSHI

Why? Why? Why? Forming the habit of asking why helps us to increase our understanding and overcome our ethnocentrism. We are unlikely to ask this critical question if we have already made a negative judgment about someone or their culture. Thus after checking and suspending our initial negative judgments, we must intentionally seek new insights into the situation to enhance our understanding.

Asking why keeps our mind open to receiving new information. It prompts us to search for answers, for understanding. We need to know more because knowing leads to understanding and empathy, which opens the door to more effective ministry with people.[11]

Below are a series of illustrations that reveal how people discovered cultural understanding by getting another's perspective. Some illustrations show the horrible results when we try to do important things without first getting the perspective of the local people.

Crushing crowds rather than lines. Having lived in South Africa for a number of years (and in Zimbabwe briefly), and having lots of experience in North American airports, I was accustomed to nice, neat lines where people patiently waited their turn. Arriving for the first time at the Manila airport, I assumed I'd find the same kinds of lines. Instead, there was this huge mass of bodies all pressing against each other trying to reach the ticket counter. Should I go to the furthest end of this mass? It would take forever. Should I try to angle in from the side? That seemed rude. Should I go to a restaurant and come back just in time to board? Only at the risk of having my seat given away. So I plunged into the crowd. At any given time there were two or three suitcases pressing against me. I tried to keep a respectful inch away from the suitcase of the person in front of me. That didn't work. People kept edging the corner of their luggage into the inch of space, and I was now obligated to let them in. Until I learned the rules and played by them, I lost ground. (Did I mention the suffocating heat?)

Carley Dodd had a similar experience in India buying a transportation ticket.

We got there early (like good Americans) and secured our place in front of the ticket window. Nobody else was around so we felt confident that our waiting would be minimal once the window opened. However, when the ticket window opened, about one hundred people came out of nowhere and crowded around us, squeezing us out of what we thought was our place in line. After a half hour of standing in the same place while everyone else crowded in front, we finally realized that is this culture there was no such thing as a "line"—it was everyone for himself. Once we understood that, we soon had our tickets.[12]

Dodd explains that many cultures of the world do not think in linear ways—in terms of straight lines. Nor do they have the same sense of personal space. These differences represent ways cultures have evolved. We might prefer one or the other way, but to survive and prosper in another culture, we must see, think and do as the nationals.

I'm yours for life. In many parts of the world the patron-client system, along with many accompanying assumptions, is deeply embedded. In North America, the patron-client relationship is encountered in anthropology books. Patrons (owners, landlords, the wealthy) hire people, called clients, to work for them. In North America we would call this an employer-employee relationship, but very different assumptions underlie the two systems, which cause serious problems.

Often, clients don't see themselves simply as employees but as faithful workers who will, until death, receive wages, health benefits and general protection from the patron. That is, clients see employment as a lifelong arrangement. Many countries have laws whereby the patrons must give these lifetime benefits to the clients. As such, the client's retirement, social security and health coverage is tied to the patron.

Missionaries and relief and development workers have discovered this accidentally. When they hire a local person for a job, the missionaries assume that this is a contract that is good for a limited time—as long as they wish to employ the person. If the missionaries are unhappy with the person's job performance, they may sever the relationship and hire someone else, believing they have no further obligation to the client (employee). However, the client took the job believing that he or she would be employed and protected for life.[13] But the fact is with many missionaries or mission agencies, the patron and client often come to the arrangement with very different sets of assumptions.

Why do other cultures operate this way? One reason is found in the financial arrangement. Most of the clients hire themselves to patrons at a very cheap wage. The reason they take a job for such cheap wages is that they assume that this is a lifetime arrangement and even though they will never get rich, they will be protected for the rest of their life. The missionary who does not understand this will be in for a surprise and maybe a lawsuit.

A Christian organization headquartered in the United States had several Westerners in the Philippines, but it also employed a sizable number of Filipinos who would have the responsibility for managing affairs in their own country. Things went relatively smoothly until the organization decided to leave the Philippines and turn all the work over to the Filipinos they had employed, assuming that they could neatly sever the patron-client relationships. The Filipinos, on the other hand, had been working rather cheaply, and they were assuming that their income, health care and security were secured for life by the American organization. Things got quite messy, including lawsuits by the Philippine government. This lack of understanding proved costly in many ways.

Do you understand? Westerners who have just given some kind of instruction or direction to a local person will usually end with, "Do you understand?" Rarely will a local person respond, "No, I don't understand"—even when they don't. This, of course, causes frustration because the lack of understanding usually reveals itself sooner or later. So why this confusion?

In shame-based cultures, a person tries to *never* respond in the negative. To say no to someone is considered harsh or rude. Furthermore, to say "I don't understand" is to imply that the person explaining was not clear. Thus we would cause this person shame or loss of face to say "I don't understand" after we have just given directions. Or the person hearing "Do you understand?" may feel shame or lose face if they really don't understand. They avoid this disgrace by answering in the affirmative. If the person saying "Do you understand" is the boss, patron or a high status person (and this is often the case), to say no would cause the client (employee) to lose face. So, the client always says, "Yes, I understand." Obviously, the consequences are usually negative, but for the moment everyone saves face.

Eunice and the roses. Eunice was a Zulu lady who worked for us when we lived in South Africa. In our front yard were dozens of rose bushes. One of Eunice's responsibilities each day during blooming season was to pick a few roses for the center of our table.

Which roses would you pick for your dining table? Where I came from, it would have been the younger roses about to burst open or the ones that had opened just that day. This made sense because these would be the most beautiful, and they would also last for a few days when placed in water. Eunice apparently didn't see it that way. The roses she brought in were the oldest, petals browning at the edges, drooping and even falling off. We had dozens of beautiful ones. Why did she pick the least attractive for our table? It irritated me, and I wondered if she was making some kind of negative statement about us. My wife didn't think so. Perhaps the Zulu view of beauty was different from ours.

Actually, we never talked to Eunice about her reasoning, fearing she may think we were unhappy with her work. But there are two plausible interpretations. Eunice may have had a different view of people than we did. She came from a collectivistic culture where people don't think as individualistically as we do in the West.[14] Beauty was to be first shared with one's community and then with one's family. Eunice, sensitive to the neighbors and those walking by, wanted them to enjoy the beautiful flowers. When the last moments of beauty came, she would pick them for the house. If a person had resources such as beautiful roses, he or she had an obligation to share that beauty with others for their enjoyment.

Another possible interpretation is that Eunice's view of beauty was different from ours. Perhaps for her, beauty was in the largeness and fullness of the flower, not in the bud or the early phases of unfolding. Beauty looks different to different people. Whereas I wondered if Eunice was making a negative statement about us in some way, maybe she was opening our eyes to another way of seeing beauty and how we could share beauty with others. Trying to understand Eunice's way of seeing helped me understand her; it caused me to be less quick to judge her and helped me make a small step toward a new perspective. When wider perspectives and broader understanding replace narrowness, we become better people.

The tricky business of generosity. Jason Saunders tells a story about gift giving.

> I constantly offered to do things for [Boli Zhiang] that he graciously refused. One time, I offered to get his computer fixed for free. He thanked me profusely yet had his computer fixed at a store. I was confused and troubled by this. Then his [friend] explained that to be in my debt, without an obvious means of returning the favor, would be, for him, a loss of face because he was ten years older than me. This meant that if I wanted to do something nice for him, I had to arrange for him to help me in some way.[15]

Jason discovered that giving a gift can be complicated, and understanding the cultural rules important. It involves age, status, saving or losing face, perceptions of gaining or losing honor, and economics (i.e., being too indebted, too obligated to another). It's just one piece of the puzzle or a loose string on the back of the tapestry until we begin to see its place in the bigger picture, then it becomes part of an integrated, cohesive whole.

Understanding changes us in ways that help us build relationships for sensitive, culturally appropriate serving or, put another way, to be Jesus wherever God puts us.

CHECK YOUR MOTIVES

Getting the other's perspective is not easy—and it's not easy because of our ethnocentrism. When we enter another culture and stay bound to our ethnocentrism, local people notice we aren't there to learn from them but to teach them; we won't ask questions but will give answers; we aren't there to be with them but to train them; we won't build trust but will attempt to transform them; we're not there to dialogue but to lecture. Paulo Freire, the Brazilian educator, calls this a "subject-object relationship." Unchecked ethnocentrism turns human beings into objects to be manipulated. Freire also says that such relationships are not

> to exchange ideas, but to dictate them; not to debate or discuss themes, but to give lectures; not to work with the student but to work on him, imposing an order to which he has had to accommodate. By giving the student formulas to receive and store, we have not offered him the means for authentic thought.[16]

When people are treated as having no dignity, the image of God they bear is profaned even further. Thus in our zeal to do the work of God, we may in fact be working against God's purposes.

The ultimate perspective is God's perspective—we should try to see things as he sees them. For example, God calls himself our Father and he calls us his children. As Father he always looks out for our best interest. He may say no to our prayers because his perspective on that situation is far better than ours; what we are asking for may hurt us. While knowing these facts growing up, it was not until I became a father that I began to get a much better grip on God's perspective. As I held our firstborn, Scott, I realized there was nothing I would not do for him.

Then I realized much more deeply that was exactly how my heavenly Father felt about me. I love my son unconditionally, the same way my heavenly Father loves me. I would sacrifice anything, even my life, in order for Scott to live. And so my heavenly Father did that for me through his Son, Jesus. I understand God's perspective on being a father, and I look for his perspective on other matters: suffering, loving my enemies, reaching a lost world, extending mercy, living justly, stewarding my time and resources.

GOING FROM THE NATURAL TO THE UNNATURAL

Everyone is ethnocentric. It's natural to believe that we do things the best way. So it's unnatural for the cross-cultural servant to assume that other cultures have been blessed by God. But when we discover the validity of other cultures' ways (though maybe not all their ways), we not only discover the beauty and diversity of God's own character, but we discover something about ourselves and are freed to change in ways that better reveal our Creator to others.

Seeing things as others see them is the way of the servant. Seeing things the way God sees them is the way of the disciple: "Pay attention to my wisdom, listen well to my words of insight" (Prov 5:1). In the Christian pilgrimage to servanthood, God's wisdom, his understanding, leads us to serving others.

SERVING
Becoming Like Christ to Others

> " 'You are my servant';
> I have chosen you and have not rejected you."
>
> ISAIAH 41:9

The following story is told by Ted Engstrom, former president of World Vision. It's a wonderful example of what someone did to try to get the perspective of another (perspective taking) and use it for serving others.

Pat Moore, who looked eighty-five years old, ventured into an unusual journey of an assumed identity. In reality she was twenty-six years old, attractive with a good job in industrial design. Her makeover into an elderly person, with all the characteristics of frailty, including a cane, fooled everyone. Pat had a longstanding concern for the aged and was now going to see what it was like—as best she could. Ted writes:

> For at least once each week for the next three years, "85-year-old" Pat put on her masquerade of facial latex foam, a heavy fabric that bound her body, and a convincing gray wig. She visited fourteen states as an old woman. She met hundreds of people who never once discovered her true identity.
>
> Remember the old saying that we never really know the needs of another until we've walked a mile in his or her moccasins? That is precisely what Pat Moore did for 36 months. She developed such

a sensitivity for the aged in our midst that she actually started to "feel" old. Her experiment was the consummate definition of complete identification with other.

Pat's successful attempt to get in touch with the needs of the aged is a living example of a vital principle in learning and living the fine art of friendship: *Always treat others as equals.*

This principle obviously does not apply only to the aged. There also needs to be a greater sense of mutual respect among the races, the sexes, our competitors, and our bosses or employees.

But would we not live wiser, happier and more fulfilled lives if we enjoyed each other for what the other person is? Young or old, black or white, rich or poor, adult or child? Treating others as equals is a keystone in learning how to be a friend.[1]

Regarding "treating others as equals," sometimes those of us from the West communicate something slightly different: "I will treat you as an equal if you treat me as your superior." We need to guard our ways so that the servant spirit we wish to portray is accurately perceived by others.

Pat entered the culture of the elderly and experienced exactly what it was like to be old. This is what Jesus did in the incarnation. He lived among humans for over thirty years. And he knew what he had to do to serve the human race: he had to die. But between the time of his birth and death, especially during the three years of his public ministry, he served in two ways: (1) calling people to repentance and faith, and (2) doing good. These are neither mutually exclusive nor necessarily attached. That is, we may do good *and* also share our faith. Or we may do good *but not* feel led to share our faith—at that time. It's not wise to exclusively do one or the other. The Scripture seems clear that we are to witness in word *and* deed, and thus serve people in both their eternal and temporal needs.

DEFINITION OF SERVING

Serving is *the ability to relate to people in such a way that their dignity as human beings is affirmed and they are more empowered to live God-glorifying lives.* First, serving always includes relationships, even if brief. Second, the servant respects those served because of their God-given dignity. Third, the persons served feel empowered because they have encountered Jesus, whether they consciously recognize him or not. They may feel respected, challenged or even confronted. Whatever the case, they feel empowered to replicate the good brought to them. Anytime we relate to others in a way that leads them to sense Jesus' presence or consider his claims, God is pleased. Jesus' followers are called to be Jesus to every human being—to serve as he served.

Serving without understanding creates confusion or worse. With the help of a cane an old Filipina woman hobbled down into the ditch alongside a road on the outskirts of Manila. An American woman watched with interest from a distance. It appeared that the old woman was in some trouble. The American woman hurried to the ditch and anxiously looked down. Sure enough the old woman appeared to be in agony, her face full of pain as she squatted in the ditch. The American woman went down the embankment to render assistance. As the woman got close, the old woman began waving her cane in a threatening manner while firing off verbal assaults. Confused but determined not to leave this suffering woman, the American good Samaritan examined the situation more closely. Only then did she realize that the old woman was having her daily "bathroom" visit and was not in need of any outside assistance.[2]

Obviously this was an innocent mistake. The American woman detected one more thread in the cultural tapestry, one more piece in the cultural puzzle. Now she knows how to interpret certain behaviors in the Philippines and will be wiser and a bit more understanding. Nonetheless, we should never hesitate to help if it seems someone is in need.

It may turn out a bit embarrassing, but sometimes the best learning comes from experience.

Americans aren't the only ones who do embarrassing things. An Asian girl, new to the West, was becoming weary and bored standing in a crowded train. She did what was perfectly acceptable in her home culture: she rested her chin on the shoulder of the stranger in front of her. The shocked look she received told her this was not a common practice in her new culture.[3]

A "Herman" cartoon reveals how lack of understanding can cause a serious problem. The scene is a prison cell. The prisoner is sitting on the floor with arms and hands tightly shackled to the wall. His outstretched feet are shackled to the floor. Then the reader's eye catches the handsaw that is cutting a hole in the floor from below to help the prisoner escape. But the person with the handsaw, not being able to see the prisoner, is unwittingly going to saw through the prisoner's legs.[4]

Though we can't see the person with the saw, it's clear that he or she is a good friend, courageous and willing to risk a lot for the prisoner. However, if the friend is successful in cutting the hole, there are dire consequences for the prisoner. The message is clear: it's difficult to serve someone unless you understand their context.

Serving while disciplining. One of my former students worked among New York teenagers who lived mostly on the street. Part of his ministry was supervising teens who came into the shelter for rehabilitation. One difficulty was how to enforce the rules without appearing superior. One day, when a boy had broken a rule, the predetermined punishment was scraping gum off the sidewalk. This was particularly humiliating because his old street buddies might see him—rubbing salt in the wound.

The supervisor, required to enforce the rules, thought hard about how to escape the serious downside to this punishment. Finally he gave the teen a putty knife and led him out to the sidewalk. Then, before the teen was able to kneel down and begin scraping the gum off the sidewalk, the supervisor pulled out a putty knife from his back pocket, kneeled down and started scraping.

Servanthood takes different forms, depending on the situation. That is why it can't be legislated, formulated or scripted in any detail. It is, after all, an attitude that, when embedded within us, finds an appropriate way to express itself in every situation. If it isn't an expression of who we are, it will come across as artificial and false.

FORGIVENESS: CHINESE AND AMERICAN STYLES

I had been giving a series of lectures at a Hawaiian university. After I had spoken on cultural values and illustrated one point on forgiveness, an articulate woman from Singapore approached me. She began to rehearse pieces of her past life with her father. He had made mistakes that had hurt her. "I pushed him and pushed him just to say, 'I'm sorry,' but he never would. If he would just say those words, then everything would be all right. I was so upset because he would never say the words," she declared with emotion.

"Often he would want to give me gifts, and I would refuse to accept them until he said he was sorry. He would offer to do other things for me, and I would always refuse until he said the words. Sometimes he would ask me to do a favor for him, and I would say "no, not until you apologize," she continued.

Several times during this conversation she would identify herself as all-American even though she was born and grew up in Singapore. She had largely rejected her Singaporean cultural values and adopted American values in a wholesale way. Thus, she appeared "all-American."

The young woman adamantly insisted that she must hear the words "I'm sorry" from her father in order for forgiveness to be genuine and the relationship to be restored. Through the years she had not budged on her demands, and her father, still in Singapore, was equally intractable. By refusing his gifts and refusing to do anything for him as a good daughter would, she was punishing him and trying to force change in her father. So far both remained stubbornly entrenched in their positions. The relationship had suffered under this strain for a number of years.

It seemed to exhaust her to tell the story. I affirmed her desire to have a renewed relationship with her father. Gently I suggested that maybe her father *was* expressing his sorrow by the gifts he was offering. Maybe he was saying that he wanted a father-daughter relationship by making the kinds of requests that fathers would make of daughters when all is well between them. I told her that in the West, forgiveness (saying "I'm sorry") is a verbal exchange. In many other cultures an apology and forgiveness are expressed through actions. "Maybe your father has been expressing his apology by the acts of gift-giving and asking favors, and you have been refusing it," I offered. Her eyes stared into space as this new idea penetrated deeply into her mind.

I continued, "You are asking him to become like you, like the Western culture you have adopted. Maybe you need to let him speak out of his own cultural context. You are asking him to do something that is very foreign and uncomfortable within his culture. He may be saying 'I'm sorry' very loudly and sincerely, but the Western ears you have adopted are unable to hear it."

She had mentioned to me earlier that her father was not a Christian in spite of her long-time witness. Now I began to wonder. At some risk I raised a question: "Is it possible that your father continues to reject Christianity because he sees it as becoming like the Westerners? Do you think he believes that to become a Christian he must reject his cultural heritage and become like a foreigner—an American?" The thought seemed to paralyze her. Her jaw slowly dropped and her eyes again stared into space. Absorbed in silence for a moment she reentered the conversation, pensively saying, "I must think about that."

That evening before the next session, she came and asked how she could rebuild her relationship with her father. This difficult but important decision would set her in a new direction because now she would enter her father's world on his cultural terms and try to see through his cultural lenses. Her newfound openness would demonstrate acceptance toward her father. Previously she could accept him only on her American terms. Now she would accept him as Singaporean. The next question focused on trust: what would rebuild trust in a way her father would understand it from his Chinese culture. Rather than force her father into her Western ways, she would try to fit into his Chinese ways, acting and reacting from his cultural frame of reference. She well understood Chinese culture, but she had rejected it as totally pagan. She had failed in trying to serve her father from her Western frame of reference. Now she resolved to serve her father from his frame of reference. That is how we truly serve.

GOING BACKWARDS MAKES THE MOST SENSE

The servanthood model has progressed along the following steps: openness, acceptance, trust, learning, understanding, serving. The model has evolved over a decade of talks with church leaders around the world, reading the Scriptures with special attention to the life of Jesus and careful examination of God's truth as found in the social science and cross-cultural communications literature. The model has been field tested in about twenty countries, and you are reading the insights of hundreds of people who have contributed to it. Now, we look at the model backwards because, as you will see, it makes the most sense that way. So please read the next piece carefully to see whether all this creates a richer perspective for you.

Serving. You can't serve someone you don't understand. At best you can only be a benevolent oppressor—like forcing someone to say "I'm sorry" when that is a an unnatural way to apologize.

Understanding. You can't understand another person until you have learned *from* them and, eventually, *with* them. A learning attitude signals humility and a willingness to identify with the people.

Learning. You can't learn from another person until you have built trust with them. People won't share important information with someone they don't trust, especially cross-culturally.

Trust. You can't build trust with another person until they feel like they have been accepted by you—until they feel that you value them as human beings.

Acceptance. You can't communicate value and esteem to others unless they feel welcomed into your presence and find themselves feeling safe—openness.

Openness. Openness with people of another culture requires that you are willing to step out of your comfort zone to initiate and sustain relationships in a context of cultural differences. While requiring some risk, it launches you on the wonderful and fruitful pilgrimage to servanthood.

Openness is rooted deeply in our view of the God who welcomes sinners and accepts them as bearers of his image; thus each person possesses a sacred dignity—the kind of dignity that compels us to also welcome others into our lives.

But we are not yet done with the model. People from other cultures who have seen the model made similar observations: The model's content is good, and it addresses issues that Westerners need to hear to be servants in our culture. However, its linear format may work for you people in the West, but it's not how our minds work. To make the model work for us, you must think in circular terms.

When I asked them to explain what they meant, they invariably came up with a schema that more comfortably fit their cultural way of thinking—an integrative circular model.

They didn't think of serving as being at the end of a progression of steps but as something that was happening whenever we are open, accepting, trusting, learning and understanding. Furthermore, they didn't

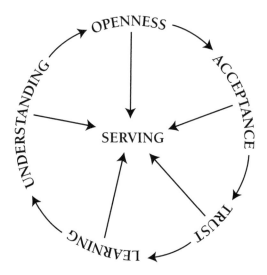

see the need to start with openness, though that is a logical place (for me) to start. A person could start serving just by learning from others. Later the person could show openness, get understanding, build trust and communicate acceptance.

The imagery used was similar to a pinball machine—serving others is like a pinball, always bouncing back and forth between the posts and bumpers (openness, understanding, trust, leaning and acceptance), not always knowing what was next but appropriately responding to the situation by being ready to display the servant spirit wherever you were. Their integrative circular ideas are wonderful and probably better reflect reality. But I still like my linear approach; it helps me make sense of the servant process in my Western way of thinking. However, for a growing number of people in the West and for most of the people in the Two-Thirds World, the circular model may make more sense. I am deeply indebted to those who taught me and patiently helped me see the circular model's advantages. Use the model that works best for you.

Part Three

SERVANTHOOD
The Challenges

THE SERVANT AND LEADERSHIP

"Alfred North Whitehead claimed that all
true education is religious education.
In the same spirit, all true leadership is religious leadership—
for religion has to do with cleansing the human self of the toxins
that make our leadership more death-dealing than life-giving."

PARKER PALMER

"Mission . . . must take the form of servanthood.
Only in this way can it escape the charge of arrogance."

G. THOMPSON BROWN

I've done a fair amount of writing in my life, and this chapter has been the most difficult. In all honesty, I find the leadership literature confusing, including that written by Christian authors. I have pastored a church, led two educational institutions and held other administrative positions—all positive experiences—but I still would rather avoid the topic of leadership.

The basic question is, How do we combine the concept of service with that of leadership? Usually we resolve this dilemma by simply joining the two like conjoined twins—servant-leadership. This easy fix really doesn't change anything. Leaders still do their thing. Some gifted leaders are prone to a dictatorial style, yet they still lay claim to the servant-leader title, though the servant part is badly distorted if not missing. Others obviously aren't gifted leaders. This creates yet other problems. Both situations are equally unbiblical and wreak destruction on the body of Christ. Unfortunately, such people rarely recognize their leadership limitations because, having thought of themselves as a servant-leader, they become convinced that they are.

I don't find the servant-leader title particularly useful. The repeated use of the word *servant* apparently doesn't sufficiently remind us of the type of leadership we are called to exercise. Many who think of themselves as a servant-leader aren't—which amounts to self-deception. Many are tyrants, dictators, self-aggrandizers and benevolent oppressors. What sometimes passes for Christian leadership is rather shocking.

The other reason I question the usefulness of *servant-leader* is that we don't create similar hybrids when discussing other gifts in the church: servant teacher, servant pray-er, servant encourager, servant helper and so on. How did the word *servant* first become attached to *leader?* Leader and leadership are rather modern inventions; they're not common in the vocabulary of Scripture. So I suspect attaching *servant* to *leader* was an attempt to correct certain abuses within the Christian community. Frankly, placing *servant* in front of *leader* sounds very spiritual but seems not to have done much good.

This chapter represents my understanding of the Scripture's teaching on the church, on being a servant, on humility, on giftedness and on the priesthood of all believers. I will apply each of them to issues of leadership.

Several things are clear. First, the Bible speaks much more about being a servant than it does about leadership. That should tell us something. Second, the Bible recognizes there are good and bad leaders, so we must expect both. Third, being trained in Scripture doesn't guarantee that a person will be a good leader. (The Pharisees were well trained but also blatant hypocrites; see Mt 23:13-36.) Fourth, God alone appoints and gifts those he wishes to lead. The church in its corporate wisdom confirms the gifts God has given, not only to a leader but also to each member.

Institutions that claim to train most everyone to be leaders may be doing a disservice to the kingdom. Joe Stowell, past president of Moody Bible Institute, says that at best only 20 percent of Moody's student body have gifts of leadership. The other 80 percent are followers.[1] Yet I know many Christian institutions who give the distinct impression that everyone will graduate as a leader. Virtually every college major and leadership-development program implies that the graduates will be fit to lead. I find this grossly misleading (pun intended), and it sets people up with false expectations. It's also bad theology since only God bestows leadership gifts (Rom 12:6; 1 Cor 12:4-6). Consequently, many have been trained to lead but are not so gifted, thus creating problems for everyone.

Fifth, people will lead according to their personality, history, role models and other influences. None of these formative influences should deny one overriding reality: all expressions of leadership must be guided by biblical principles.

Many of those who believe their education has equipped them for leadership become missionaries. How does this belief affect their expectations about their role in the new culture? How does it play out with people who are already leaders in that culture? Is leadership as it is practiced in the West a good model for other cultures? These questions are hard to answer, and indeed they should be. Perhaps we are using the wrong model. Given the dominance of *service* and *humility* in Scripture, maybe we ought to be asking more questions about what a servant looks like.

Since my brief comments will not change the vocabulary we use, I will continue to use *leader* and *leadership*, but the terms will be recast and nuanced differently by what we have previously examined and now applied to our understanding of biblical leadership.

THE TRADITIONAL TRIBAL CHIEF

Some years ago, I was the acting director of a missionary training organization and on a committee seeking a new CEO. This person would be our leader for the foreseeable future, so leadership style became an important issue. I asked one candidate whether he could give me a metaphor of his style of leadership. Previous interviewees used coach-and-team or orchestra-and-conductor metaphors; one used a cheerleader metaphor. But this person offered a striking metaphor that I believe better represented kingdom values.

He described the role of the traditional tribal chief. He noted that we rarely see this type of chief anymore. Yet the metaphor captured his view of leadership. The traditional chief would call the elders of the village together and describe the problem, challenge an issue that needed to be resolved. The elders would sit in a circle around the fire. While the chief may wear some symbol of leadership, he joined the circle as an equal. The chief knew the elders had done their duty of listening to the people and were sensitive to the pulse of the village. He was confident they would voice the wisdom of the people.

As the chief shared with the elders, he was careful to present all the information relevant to the topic. He didn't signal any predisposition toward a right answer or a preferred decision. He then opened the forum for discussion. The elders would speak, listen, question and probe, attempting to see things from all perspectives. Taking a position on the matter wasn't important because that would hinder due process. It was important that everyone feel safe to speak, to share their perspectives and insights. On rare occasions the discussion might last for days. Eventually a consensus would surface among them. Some would begin to think in a certain direction. Others soon saw the wisdom and joined in with their support.

When the chief realized that all supported a particular direction, he would stand to announce the decision to all. They didn't need to hear it, since it had been obvious for some time. Yet they needed to hear it from their leader to be sure that he accurately represented the wisdom of the group.

Obviously, not everyone would be equally enthusiastic about the decision, but all were committed to supporting it because their voices had been respected in the process. Thus they were able to share their ideas without losing face or feeling shame. Sharing information and a variety of perspectives was valued more than getting one's own viewpoint adopted. Often, so many voices and so much information emerged that it was hard to tell whose position prevailed. The strength of a process that involves everyone is that everyone helps make the decision. When people come to a discussion with open minds and not with predetermined positions, competition, jealousy and turfing (the protection of one's own territory) are kept to a minimum.

The Western leader often makes decisions in isolation and then asks, How can I get the others to own it? This often doesn't work, and rarely do others feel ownership. This may account for the difficulty missionaries experience when nationals are slow to get involved or lack enthusiasm for a new idea. People who own a decision will work for its success, but they will be less enthusiastic when a leader tries to sell them a predetermined decision.

Once the chief had announced the decision to the other elders and saw their heads nod in approval, he would then gather the villagers together and announce the decision to them. Each village family, seeing that their trusted representative concurred with the decision, welcomed the words of the chief and immediately set about their responsibilities in carrying out the decision. Now everyone was involved in and committed to a successful outcome of the decision.

The chief's role was to oversee the outworking of the decision. He would clarify any questions, make sure resources were available, and encourage and do whatever was necessary for the elders and villagers to fulfill their tasks. More importantly, the villagers were confident that the elders' decision would serve the good of the entire village.

Back to our search committee: The person who told this story was hired and served us well. He wonderfully modeled the values of the tribal chief.

A REALITY CHECK

The leadership style of the traditional African tribal chief is sometimes called the consensus style. Its effectiveness depends on several factors: the leader is respected but not feared; people are willing to honestly and openly engage the topic; everyone is committed to the good of the larger body while minimizing or setting aside personal ambitions; everyone trusts each other; most of the decision-makers have the trust of the larger community and have heard the wisdom of the populace. Some sense of egalitarianism should exist. There are many places in the world where this style would be considered folly. In many former Soviet Union countries, of course, the dictatorial, heavy-handed, authoritarian leadership style still prevails even in many churches. We must be slow to judge because it seems that style was necessary and effective during the communist era. In other places, though, leadership positions are used to consolidate power, exploit others and enjoy excess privilege.

The situation is far from hopeless, and I think it's improving. As the biblical values of the servant inform and influence leadership styles, pastors are responding appropriately. In South Africa I know of pastors who are working to accept others because in so doing they honor Christ. They are spending more time building trust with board members and are finding that it increases communication and clarifies motives. A spirit of cooperation and humility are in greater evidence. Meetings are characterized by more laughter and energized conversation; the wisdom of others is sought, and ultimately churches are finding God's own wisdom. People leave the meetings nurtured and encouraged, eager to take their servant spirit back to all members of the church and community.

THE LEADER'S RESPONSIBILITY

Modeling Christ. The leader's first and foremost responsibility is to model the servanthood of Christ. By that standard all expressions of leadership must be measured.

Everyone is called to be a servant. This is the foremost calling of all who decide to follow Jesus. The leader, however, has the particular responsibility of showing the people of God what that servant life looks like. The religious leaders of Jesus' day got this completely wrong (see Mt 23:1-36), and right up to the end of Jesus earthly life the disciples also got it wrong (see Mt 20:20-28). No individual leader will capture all of what Jesus was, but every leader must show us something of what Jesus was. And it seems that every leader must evidence the essence of Jesus: humility.

The humble servant. Humility is the chief characteristic of the servant. Because humility is so central to serving others, we do well to hear God's own voice regarding it:

> Remember how the LORD your God led you all the way in the desert these forty years, to humble you. . . . He humbled you, . . . to teach you. (Deut 8:2-3)

> Pride goes before destruction,
>   a haughty spirit before a fall.
> Better to be lowly in spirit and among the oppressed
>   than to share plunder with the proud. (Prov 16:18-19)

> He has showed you O man, what is good.
>   And what does the LORD require of you?
> To act justly and to love mercy
>   and to walk humbly with your God. (Mic 6:8)

> The greatest among you will be your servant. For whoever exalts himself will be humbled, and whoever humbles himself will be ex-

alted. (Mt 23:11-12; see also Prov 15:33; 18:12; Is 2:9, 11; 5:15;
10:33; Mt 18:4; Lk 14:11; 18:14; 1 Pet 5:6)

All of you, clothe yourselves with humility toward one another,
    because,
  "God opposes the proud
      but gives grace to the humble." (1 Pet 5:5)

Humility is mostly expressed in relationships. There does seem to be
a priority though. Humility before God generates humility toward others. If humility toward others is not evident, it's unlikely we see ourselves
correctly before God. To see God clearly is to see how unworthy we are.
Harboring pride is a way of saying "I am worthy of the good things happening around me. I take the credit—the glory." At this point God stands
in opposition to such people because they, in their pride, rob God of the
glory he deserves. Perhaps this is why God uses some of his most provocative language to impress on us the necessity of humility and the dangers of pride.[2] Humility is the core attitude of the servant who is gifted
to lead.

DOCTRINES INFORMING THE SERVANT GIFTED TO LEAD

The priesthood of all believers is a guiding doctrine for the servant who
would lead. Like the Old Testament priests, Christians have two over-
arching relationships: a vertical relationship with God, whereby we com-
mune with him through our high priest, Jesus, and an horizontal relationship with all people, whereby we mediate God's grace and mercy to
each other. Only, says Larry Richards, "when we realize that each believer is to be discipled and to disciple, to be ministered to and to minister, can we understand the role of leadership."[3]

The head of a church, mission or other Christian organization is its
leader because God, we assume, has made that appointment and has
graciously bestowed appropriate gifts. That appointment and those gifts

have one purpose: to serve God by serving others. But other people also have gifts; in fact every member of the body has at least one gift by which to serve others. In order for the body to function properly, every member must receive from the giftedness of others and give out of their own giftedness (Rom 12:5-8; 1 Cor 12:12-29). This describes the priestly function. We all minister and are ministered to. We all disciple and are discipled. The leader who lacks humility will have difficulty with seeing all believers as priests and will fail to connect with them in ways that their priestly roles can be mutually beneficial. This humble exercise of gifts among the church's holy priesthood has several implications:

1. The gifts of leadership must be exercised in community.

2. Leaders must be open to receiving ministry from differently gifted people.

3. Leaders must demonstrate acceptance toward all members of the body of Christ because though gifted differently, they have value as God's image-bearers and can mediate (minister) God's grace to one another.

4. Leaders must show openness and build trust with others so everyone will feel free to minister their own gifts to all others, including the leaders.

5. Leaders must be attentive to the voice of the people, learning from and with them so that their collective wisdom can be garnered for making wise decisions.

6. Leaders must understand the tapestry of the people's lives, feel their pain, celebrate their joys and walk with them on their journey so that the exercise of the leaders' gifts become tuned and fitted for the hearts and experiences of the people.

7. Leaders must realize that vision casting and decision making will be most effective when done in the context of implications 1-6. Excluded from the wisdom of the community, leaders are cut off from

the wisdom of God as expressed through his people. It's like the monkey making decisions about what is in the best interests of the fish (see "The Monkey 'Serves' the Fish" in chapter 3). The leader, whose first calling is to model the servanthood of Christ, listens carefully to others, seeks their insights and carefully weighs their thoughts.

While I think these points apply to all Christian leaders, let's focus on cross-cultural servanthood. The leader who serves will be a good listener, probing often and deeply the wisdom of others in the local community. Good listening skills affirm those we are ministering to, and subsequently they will be more willing to share their lives with us and vice versa. Listening also signals humility, a willingness to be taught by the other. In most cultures outside the West, this will take considerable time. People love to linger in conversation at a café, under a shade tree or over tea. Western ideas of appointments and schedules must give way to the unhurried lives of the local people.

I am deeply disturbed by leaders who isolate themselves in their study for most of the week, spending little time being with people, and then deliver exegetically correct and rhetorically powerful sermons that are irrelevant to the person in the pew. The same is true for organizational leaders who are preoccupied with conferences, trips and "important" meetings but who rarely take time to listen to their employees. Then these leaders announce decisions that are not grounded in the reality of the workplace. I find unilateral decision making at any level to be based on a faulty view of self, the church, the image of God and the priesthood of all believers. Such leadership often marginalizes the people who carry the workload and finally descends into despotism. This descent becomes even more swift and horrific when it happens in another culture where the leader has never bothered to learn very much *from* or *with* the people.

I am deeply disturbed by the leader who, removed from the influence of others, receives a vision from God for the future and then autocratically delivers it to the masses. Does God speak only to leaders? Has God exhausted his wisdom only on people with titles? Can anyone else hear the voice of God or receive his vision? If so, would the leadership listen? Does any of this make sense in light of the priesthood and the giftedness of all believers? Didn't God make us a body, a fellowship, a community? Hasn't God called for leaders to be humble servants? Aren't artificial titles to be banished in the church (Mt 23:5-12)? Didn't Jesus say, "You are all brothers" (Mt 23:8)?

Francis Schaeffer aptly observes:

> The basic relationship between Christians is not that of elder and people, or pastor and people, but that of brothers and sisters in Christ. This denotes that there is one Father in the family and that his offspring are equal. There are different jobs to be done, different offices to be filled, but we as Christians are equal before one Master. We are not to seek a great title: we are to have the places together as brethren.[4]

This too translates into the cross-cultural situation, whether into another ethnic community or another country. When missionaries are taught that *they* are the leaders and *they* alone are equipped to do leadership, they think they will do vision casting and decision making in the new culture. But maybe some preliminary questions should be asked. Are all missionaries automatically leaders? Most? A few? If there are no local leaders (and we must be very cautious before stating this), then what kind of leadership might the missionary exhibit that does not violate cultural patterns?[5] Should missionaries look for local people who exhibit a Western style of leadership before trusting them? Should missionaries who have only a year or two of experience in a new culture train local leadership? Won't the trainees look Western unless missionaries have intentionally embedded themselves in the culture? I confess that I cringe whenever I hear a new missionary talk about training the nationals for leadership. Does anyone else see this as presumptuous and arrogant? What do the local people think when they see this happening?

Additionally, vision casting and decision making are always grounded in a context. The monkey got his ideas and plan of action from his own monkey context, which did not fit the context of the fish. The monkey's servanthood, in reality, was oppression. The missionary who brings a vision to the new culture will probably be seen like the monkey, well-meaning but out of touch and misguided. Unless the missionary faithfully exercises the principles of servanthood, it will be difficult to see him or her as a servant.

PAUL AND BARNABAS

Much has been said about the apostle Paul, but one point often overlooked is the temporary nature of his missionary activity. His missionary stays were for relatively short periods of time. I don't think that was the model for all to follow, but I wonder if Paul chose that because he knew he was a natural leader, a take-charge person, and unless he moved on he would hinder the emergence of local leadership. Because no church existed in the places Paul went, his own leadership was important. But as soon as he could, Paul appointed local leaders and then left, though he did stay in contact with them. There is risk in staying for a relatively short time, but Paul seemed willing to take the risk, probably for the benefit of the emerging leaders.

While Paul is often used as the model of leadership, I think Barnabas is a better model for the contemporary mission situation. While Paul was primarily evangelizing and planting and organizing churches (these gifts are still needed), Barnabas was more versatile, helping out as the situation required. He sold his property and gave it to the Christian community (Acts 4:36-37); he was sent by the church in Jerusalem to help out with the growing church in Antioch of Syria (Acts 11:19-22) and saw considerable success (Acts 11:24); he recruited Paul to help in Antioch (Acts 11:26) and then helped out with famine relief back in Jerusalem. Placing Barnabas's name before Paul's (Saul) in verse 26 suggests he had a primary leadership role during this time. Barnabas stuck with young John Mark when Paul rejected him (Acts 13:13). It was said of Barnabas, "He was a good man, full of the Holy Spirit and of faith" (Acts 11:24).

The contemporary missionary entering another culture would do well to model the versatile and supportive role seen in Barnabas. The church is well established in many parts of the world with good leadership in place. Our call may be to support rather than to lead. If we do have leadership gifts, they will be seen in our servant spirit and supportive roles. If local people are so inclined to affirm us as leaders, then so be it. But then it will be because we have first been seen as a servant. In my wife's international work, she rehearses a wonderful story that illustrates servant leadership. She says:

> When I was directing several child survival programs for World Relief, I visited Honduras and spent several days with Dr. Orestes Zuniga and his staff—all committed Christians. We visited the health promoters as they assessed the children's growth and taught mothers how to keep their children healthy in the face of great poverty. Early on in my visit, as I was observing a group of mothers sitting on low benches listening to their health promoter, I glanced around for Dr. Zuniga. It took me a while to find him. He was sitting on a couple of bricks behind the last row of women, listening intently. The health promoter, a small middle-aged woman introduced him and asked him to say a few words to the mothers.
>
> Having heard about the prevalence of machismo in Latin men, especially men with professional stature, I expected this medical doctor to expound more fully on the health topic of the day. Instead, he came forward, put his arm around the little health pro-

moter and said something to this effect: "I am so pleased to be able to hear Maria (the health promoter) teach you today. She is a wise woman who knows how to keep your children alive and well. Listen carefully to her and follow her advice." And he sat back down on his little stack of bricks behind the back row. My respect for Dr. Zuniga deepened significantly that day.

During the rest of my visit I watched this very skilled physician constantly celebrate and encourage the other members of his child-survival team. No matter how small each person's role on the team, he always commented on their important contribution, and I never remember him speaking about his own role in what was a large and hugely successful child-survival program that served many thousands of women and thousands more infants and children. Many adults today, without even knowing it, owe their very lives to the way that man lead his team of health promoters in teaching moms how to care for their little ones.

Like the other gifts, leadership is a gift given by God (1 Cor 12:12) which is to be exercised in humility, under the authority of the Holy Spirit and for the common good. Biblical leadership always points us to the servant nature of Christ and draws us to him and to live as he did.

SUMMARY

My intention has not been to give a long discourse on the servant who is gifted to lead. I did intend to create a way of thinking about leadership that is informed by important biblical doctrines. If we servants emerge as leaders as well, let it be because people have seen the servant attitude and wish to affirm our giftedness. Then it won't be a role we have assigned to ourselves but one honorably bestowed by others.

12

THE SERVANT AND POWER

"Jesus came to show us what life in the kingdom looked like,
not how to modify how the world did things."

C. GENE WILKES

"He did not desire to dominate men; He desired only to serve men.
He did not desire His own way; He desired only God's way."

WILLIAM BARCLAY

Early in my missionary career I experienced power and failed miserably in my use of it. It happened in the flow of life and didn't seem noteworthy at the time. Yet it's in the small, sometimes mundane things that we discover ourselves—our real selves. Eunice, a Zulu lady, knocked on our door. We needed house help, and she needed work. Furthermore she was recommended by someone we knew. Unemployment among black South Africans was very high. Poverty was pervasive.

That put me in a position of power—I was hiring and she needed a job.

As my wife and I talked with Eunice, I kept negotiating her down in salary, using as leverage the fact that we could easily find someone else. Knowing she might not get the job would put pressure on her to take the lowest salary. We finally agreed on a salary, and Eunice was hired. I felt good. I grew up where good negotiating skills brought respect. Also it was good stewardship to protect God's money. And I felt good because we gave a job to Eunice, who desperately needed it. But I didn't realize at the time how perverted this was. I had ways of rationalizing what I had done, which temporarily appeased my conscience. Eventually I realized God is not fooled by my word games.

As you already realize, there was nothing biblical about what I did. In fact, it was abusive and oppressive. But it was consistent with the literature of the *Harvard Business Review,* where leaders are told to use "power to influence the thoughts and actions of other people."[1]

I exercised power in a way that benefited me and worked to the disadvantage of another human being mired in poverty, without power and now further victimized. In addition to using power in the service of others, it should also be used in the service of justice (not that the two are unrelated). Had I been concerned for justice, a frequent biblical theme, how would I have handled that situation differently? Can you paint a scenario that would have made this situation an example of a *servant's* use of power?

Rather than pondering how I might serve Eunice, a human being made in the image of God, I used my power to my advantage and to her disadvantage. Instead of asking how I might be an instrument of God's righteousness (same word for justice in Mt 6:33), I obtained the best deal I could.

I have often wished I could have done it over and done it differently. I wish I could find Eunice and apologize. Apartheid, the system of whites controlling people of color in South Africa at that time, had already crushed her in every possible way; now I added to her burden. Over the following year I slowly realized that the spirit of apartheid also inhabited me. Living with the injustices of apartheid in the country was hard; acknowledging the apartheid within me was even harder.

Power is to be used in the service of others and only secondarily, if at all, for the benefit of oneself. With Eunice I violated that principle. The servant's exercise of power should increase mutual openness, acceptance and trust. Godly exercise of power always elevates the body of Christ or the local community. Power is meant to be shared with the goal of empowering others. Hoarded power weakens others and exalts oneself. Power, when grounded in biblical values, serves others by liberating them. It acknowledges that people bear the image of God and treats them in a way that will nurture the development of that image. In so doing, we honor their Creator.

THE EXERCISE OF POWER

My own thinking on leadership and power is evolving. The preceding chapters serve as the context for the exercise of power by a servant. Let's not be naive. Anyone from the West who enters a new culture (or ethnic group) has power: finances, education, resources, technology, relational networks and a passport. That power provokes less awe in the minds of many around the world these days, but it is nonetheless a position of power. I'm not so concerned about the fact that Westerners possess power; I am concerned about how it is exercised—the focus of this chapter.

Power is for service. Maxie Dunnam says:

> The way most of us serve keeps us in control. We choose whom, when, where and how we will serve. We stay in charge. Jesus is calling for something else. He is calling us to be servants. When we make this choice, we give up the right to be in charge. The amazing thing is that when we make this choice we experience great freedom. We become available and vulnerable, and we lose our fear of being stepped on, or manipulated, or taken advantage of. Are not these our basic fears? We do not want to be in a position of weakness.[2]

Dunnam makes some noteworthy points. Would you mind reading this quotation again and noting one or two points that are most important for you to ponder? My own thoughts follow:

- Everyone of us is a servant to everyone else, all the time and in every circumstance because servanthood is a state of being before it is a state of doing.

- By choosing to be a servant, we relinquish power, control and unilateral decision making in favor of listening, learning and understanding, and emerge with a decision that reflects the wisdom of God and his people.

- Contrary to human logic but consistent with the logic of the cross, glorious freedom flourishes within the servant.

- When we serve, we will be misunderstood, manipulated and abused, but will not fear, for Christ walked that same path and now walks with us.

- We will serve imperfectly. Often we don't see our own pride, our own need to control or our own willfulness. The old nature (and Satan) seeks to pervert our desire to follow Christ as humble, obedient servants. So we pray for one another and encourage one another.

The Gentile virus. Jesus said:

> You know that the rulers of the Gentiles lord it over them, and their high officials exercise authority over them. Not so with you. Instead whoever wants to become great among you must be your servant, and whoever wants to be first must be your slave—just as the Son of Man did not come to be served, but to serve, and to give his life a ransom for many. (Mt 20:25-28)

Jesus is comparing the Gentile model of leadership with the kingdom model. Wilkes notes that Jesus, in referring to the Gentile leaders, used the word *regarded*—"those who are regarded as rulers"—suggesting they did not represent the kind of leadership he was seeking from them.[3] They were following the model exhibited by the Roman occupiers: leadership that exercises power *over*; that sees people as servants; that accrues status, wealth, power and privilege; that sees people as a means to an end. Not only did Roman leaders lord it over others, they enjoyed it! I wonder if we in the mission community have also been infected with the "Gentile virus." Maybe not in such obvious ways but perhaps more subtle "Christianized" forms.

The Gentile virus also infects church leadership. While speaking to the crowds, including his disciples, Jesus turned his focus on the religious leaders of the day—the teachers of the law and the Pharisees. These powerful people exercised enormous but unfortunate influence over the religious community. Their leadership was oppressive because it followed the ungodly Gentile model.

While their knowledge of the truth was correct ("You must obey them," Mt 23:3), they used their position to lord it over their listeners. Their power was used to elevate their status and garner privilege to themselves. Read Matthew 23:1-10 and list the ways the teachers of the law and the Pharisees abused power.

Those in the church who employ the Gentile style of leadership often use biblical words, the pretense of spirituality. Over time, however, people realize that the words mask a style of leadership that lacks biblical integrity ("Do not do what they do, for they do not practice what they preach," Mt 23:3). Such failure in integrity prompted one of Jesus' greatest condemnations: "Woe to you . . . you hypocrites" is repeated time and again (Mt 23:13-29). Then Jesus uses some of the most provocative language in the Bible: "You shut the kingdom of heaven in men's faces" (v. 13), "blind guides" (v. 16), "you have neglected the more important matters" (v. 23), "full of greed and self-indulgence" (v. 25).

> *"Nearly all men can stand adversity, but if you want to test a man's character, give him power."*
>
> ABRAHAM LINCOLN

Jesus calls them (and us) to abandon the Gentile exercise of power where everything feeds into one's own comfort, status, authority and position (Mt 23:4-10). Rather, "the greatest among you will be your servant," a servant driven by a humble spirit (Mt 23:11-12). Servant leadership always ends up being other-centered: serving them and building them up (unlike the way I negotiated with Eunice). Furthermore, the servant's rhetoric is consistent with their behavior. While the "hypocrite" resides within all of us, a servant refuses to cultivate it. Such a person cultivates character and integrity instead. Since being a person of integrity is most difficult among those who know us best, the authentic life of the servant must begin at home—especially for church leaders (1 Tim 3:1-10; Tit 1:6-9).

If hypocrisy is within all of us to some degree, and if we want to be intentional about building the kind of integrity where our words match our deeds, then let's be honest with ourselves. I shared with you my hypocrisy in hiring Eunice. I'm sure she would have scoffed at the idea that I was in South Africa to serve others. Now, I challenge you to think about yourself. As you enter another culture, as you live in another culture, where are the inconsistencies between your words and deeds?

When relatives get involved. Remember when the mother of James and John came with her two sons and together[4] they asked a favor of Jesus: "Let one of us sit at your right and the other at your left in your glory" (Mk 10:37). It would appear that the Gentile virus had infected them. Jesus declares they are following the wrong model. The Gentile model adopts values contrary to Jesus' and to the church he is building. "You know that those who are regarded as rulers of the Gentiles lord it over them, and their high officials exercise authority over them. Not so with you" (Mk 10:42-43).

Since the other disciples showed indignation at James and John (Mk 10:41), it would seem they were all infected! But are any of us free of this virus? As cross-cultural workers, think about Jesus' words "Not so with you." Ours is a different way. We follow a different model of leadership. Our use of power is different. But the Gentile model is more attractive because it appeals to our pride, our base desires, our craving for prominence, for a spot in "Who's Who." Fight the Gentile virus, Jesus is saying. His followers will not lead as the Gentiles do. They follow the way of the cross—humble, obedient servanthood.

A common problem. Many missionaries and short-term workers who serve in other cultures find that the local people prevail upon them to provide the vision, take the leadership, make decisions and generally take charge. These situations have become less common, but they are still prevalent. There may be several motives driving this, and these should be clarified. One motive, I believe, is the desire to elevate the status of the guest in their culture. As a matter of cultural courtesy, the guest should be properly honored. The local people do this by encouraging the missionary to take leadership roles. Experience suggests that this is a cultural form of flattery, but it's not a genuine offer for the missionary to take charge. Because the local people may seem convincing, the missionary gives in and assumes leadership. We need to examine this practice. How can we determine when it's an acceptable cultural practice that the missionary should accept as a form of honor and then politely and gratefully refuse, and when it's a legitimate request for the leadership gifts of the missionary?

Are there other motives than honoring? Is it possible that some people use such ingratiating activity to build status by being with a higher status foreigner? I was on faculty of a Bible college in South Africa that was held in high esteem. When I became the principal of the school, many students, pastors and church leaders wanted to have their picture taken with me. I was the same person as when I was on the faculty, but now I had higher status. My feelings of significance were deflated, though, when some mature people told me that many people used the pictures to build their own status and increase their power base. Who you know and who you stand next to is a way of elevating yourself. I'm not so sure I am free of this in my own culture. How about you?

Compassionate justice. We tend to see righteousness as primarily a vertical relationship between God and people. But this is only half the picture. Righteousness in Scripture also has a horizontal dimension—we must be righteous with one another in all of our relationships, even with strangers. Sometimes we confuse righteousness and justice, believing that righteousness has to do with right relationship with God and justice with right relations with each other. From this point of view *righteousness* is vertical and a spiritual matter; *justice* is horizontal and a civil matter. However, the Scripture makes no such distinction; the same word is used for righteousness and justice. Thus "seek first his kingdom and his righteousness, and all these things will be given to you as well" (Mt 6:33) could just as accurately read "seek first his kingdom and his justice . . ." Being right with God can't be divorced from being right with others. So the prophet Micah scolds the leaders of Israel "who despise justice and distort all that is right" (Mic 3:9) through their abuse of power. Such behavior distorts God's own character in the minds of the people. Judgment, according to Micah, looms for those who persist in evil and wickedness, those acting unjustly toward people under their leadership (Mic 3:6-12). But those who follow God's law are "to act justly and to love mercy and to walk humbly with . . . God" (Mic 6:8).

Since righteousness (justice) is grounded in the very character of God (Deut 32:4-5; Ps 7:9; 2 Tim 4:8; 1 Jn 2:1), if we want to be Godlike, justice must be part of our character. Thus, when God's people (the righteous) act justly toward others (whether righteous or unrighteous), they reveal the kind of person God is and the kind of relationship he desires with people everywhere (Mt 6:1-4; Tit 3:5; 1 Jn 3:7; Rev 19).

Had this knowledge been an essential part of my own thinking and acting, I would have treated Eunice differently. Instead of drawing on my culture, where I learned to negotiate for the "best deal," I would have asked, "What will reveal the righteousness of God to Eunice? What would a just employer-employee relationship look like? How do I exercise my power in a way that I serve Eunice and she feels served? What is the right way to treat another human being?"

A missionary kid, Gordon, told me about frequently seeing an upside-down car in a gully when he rode with his parents back and forth to their home. On one occasion he noticed that there were people living in the car, and the destitute family was exposed to the winter cold, often below freezing, because the car had no windows. Other missionaries traveled the same route and had to have seen the family's situation. Yet no one did anything, which caused him to wonder what it meant to be a Christian. Is this a situation similar to the priest and Levite passing by on the other side of the road when seeing the Samaritan who had been robbed and beaten (Lk 10:30-37)? I can't judge, but we must be careful not to separate our righteousness in Christ with our living righteously and justly in this world.

Earlier I talked about riding with a missionary in Guatemala. His area had experienced a devastating earthquake a few months earlier. I asked how he responded to that disaster. He noted that the earthquake had come at a most inopportune time. His church was putting up a sign on the roof of the building advertising evangelistic meetings. The earthquake caused the sign to fall and the meetings had to be cancelled, he lamented. "So did you or the church get involved in the rescue or reconstruction efforts?" I inquired. "No, we just got on with our work. Well, there was a widow who had a crack in her wall, and we helped patch it up." I couldn't help but wonder how the community saw the church at its moment of need.

I am aware that mission agencies tend to see disaster response and community development issues as the responsibility of relief and development agencies such as World Vision and World Relief. The church should be involved in evangelism, discipleship and church planting. Such reasoning splits the vertical (righteousness with God) and the horizontal (righteous living in all our relationships). While relief and development agencies can respond in greater measure with greater resources and expertise, it seems the church must also reveal the full righteousness of God and his concern for the spiritual and physical well-being of all people. Otherwise we may present a God who is unconcerned about the whole person and thus distort the gospel.

THE BIBLICAL EXERCISE OF POWER

Biblical power looks an awful lot like Jesus as he lived the servant life—not as he lived his Lord and Christ life. In his servant life we see his ability to draw people close and make them feel safe (openness). We see his acceptance of sinners and his care for the outcasts. We see the trust he built with people and the trust he asks of us. We see how he learned about being human and grew in wisdom. He lived among us and grieved as he experienced sin's bondage of the human race. Then, it became clear that he would provide the greatest service of all: giving his own life to break the sin bondage and offer life to all who would put their trust in him. That was Jesus' leadership—being the humble, obedient servant. Our Lord became a slave to all. And millions follow his leadership today, worshiping him as Lord of the universe.

In summary:

- Leadership and power begin with being the servant of God in the spirit of serving others.

- The gift of leadership is exercised with a profound humility that reveals a proper respect for God, for oneself and for others.

- Humble leaders suspend their agenda, vision and personal wishes and listen to the wisdom of God through his people. Though this is much harder in the cross-cultural context, biblical principles and skills make it possible for all leaders.

- Engaging the people of God in respectful, mutual listening and speaking not only reveals God's wisdom but also gives them legitimate ownership in the ministry.

- People who feel ownership in a ministry naturally support the decisions of the leaders and trust them to act in the best interests of the people.

- Leaders who follow biblical principles find it easier to enlist and to empower people for the task at hand.

When the task is accomplished, the people will say "We have done it," and the leaders will happily agree and add, "By God's grace and for his glory."

THE SERVANT AND MYSTERY

"Has God's face ever been on a coin?
We are the coin that bears the living likeness of God.
Giving of ourselves with whatever that may include,
is the only legal currency of the kingdom of heaven."

GORDON AND GLADIS DEPREE

Had someone explained mystery to me in my younger days, it might have helped me handle some tough experiences I could make no earthly sense of. The apostle Paul uses the word *mystery* about twenty-one times. He often uses it to refer to the hidden purposes of God (see Rom 11:25; 1 Cor 14:2).[1] That is, God doesn't always explain the "why" to life's more vexing problems. This is a mystery to us.

FOGGY TODAY, SUNNY TOMORROW

Sometimes God allows us to see his purposes rather quickly, as in the case of Mike. A teenage missionary kid, Mike lived with us in South Africa during the school year. One day he announced he would represent his school in a track competition. This surprised me since Mike was very short for his age. But he had made the decision, and we all encouraged him. What harm could it do? He rigorously practiced and the night of the race arrived. It was in the stadium where horse races were normally held. The bright lights created a surreal effect. Other missionary kids couldn't come with Mike and me because of schedule conflict. The last race of the

evening would be Mike's. Being his first track meet, he took his time getting onto the field, and he ended up with the far outside position, a considerable disadvantage since this was not a staggered start for the three-
quarter mile race. Mike didn't seem to notice. The gun went off.

Mike stayed with the tail end of the pack into the first turn. By the
mid-way mark his short legs simply couldn't keep up. I secretly thought
it would be smart for Mike to angle off into the shadows and "disappear;"
he could meet me behind the bleachers, and we could sneak home. *Let's
save ourselves total embarrassment,* I thought. Mike's mind apparently
worked differently as he kept plodding along, falling ever further behind. When all the other runners had crossed the finish line to the polite
applause of the spectators, Mike was coming into the far turn. Looking
down from the stands, he seemed so small, so alone, so disgraced.

Whatever Mike felt, his feet just kept churning toward the finish line
to the light applause of those who remained. At the finish line a few
school friends offered feeble encouragement, but Mike slumped, head
down, shuffling dejectedly toward the stands, where we would meet. To
add to the humiliation of the evening, Mike and I had to push my little
car to get it going, much to the quizzical looks of his friends buzzing by
in their pricey models. I found no words that would fit this situation. As
we approached home, Mike mumbled, "I'm never going to enter another
race as long as I live."

Before bed, Mike requested that I give him permission to stay home
from school the next day. I offered Mike words of comfort, but he was
inconsolable. I sympathetically responded, "I think you better go to
school tomorrow," which produced a twisted face in Mike and a mourn-
ful moan. Then with primal urgency Mike pleaded, "Please, please,
please, Uncle Duane, don't make me go to school tomorrow."

Mike was in the fog. Mystery descended heavily, and I had watched it
envelop him. I had the power to postpone the misery of further humiliation. Mike sensed I was teetering and repeated his plea with greater fer-

vency. His desperation nearly overcame my resolve. I don't know what made me do it, but I said, "Mike I can think of no valid reason why you shouldn't go to school tomorrow, except that it will be hard." With drooped head he left the room.

The next morning Mike was a physical and emotional wreck. In protesting silence he ate and left with his friends for school. Disaster loomed—because now he would have to face his school mates and relive his humiliation. Losing the race the way he did was enough; now he had to face their torment.

The day started with all the school gathering in the auditorium, where the headmaster would announce the winners of the previous night. They would parade as heroes across the stage to the cheers of all. Mike tried to disappear near the back of the auditorium. As the cheers for the last hero were fading, the headmaster said something like this. "There is yet one more recognition I would like to make. One person from our school did not win a race but represented the school in our finest tradition. He, as much as any winner, made us proud. When it was clear he would not win the race, he kept on going. When many of us would have given up, he stayed the course. He finished the race. Mike, please come forward. I am proud to shake your hand." The student body erupted with thunderous cheers and clapping with calls of "Jolly good, Mike" and "Good show, ole chap!" When Mike came home, he declared it was the best day of his life.

In failure and humiliation, Mike became the school's biggest hero. The fog lifted. The mystery became known. Mike had done his best. God wrote the rest of the story.

TEN YEARS OF FOG

Sometimes God takes longer to lift the fog. One young missionary, Chuck, found the first couple years on the mission field challenging but adventurous and delightful. As he got more and more into the culture he found himself spending increasing time with the local people. The enjoyment seemed mutual, and the local people began to share deeply from their hearts, just as he did. Chuck shared what he was learning with his missionary colleagues. The colleagues wondered why they had not had a similar response since they had been there much longer.

After a couple years Chuck and his wife began inviting the local people into their home. They invited the older pastors first, knowing this was how to show respect. Eventually the younger people were included. He knew that many missionaries didn't invite the local people into their homes, but he wasn't sure why. So he kept on. Furthermore, in this culture, the local people usually came in the back door of the missionary's house—the door that servants used. They would wait there or sometimes be invited in to sit for a few moments until the business could be transacted. Chuck failed to understand why the back door should be required for the pastors and other local people. So he brought his local guests in through his front door, seating them in his living room. At the appropriate time they would gather around the table and all would eat together.

Relationships broadened and grew stronger. However, the young missionary didn't realize he was violating an unwritten rule among his missionary colleagues—"It's best not to get too familiar with them." Missionaries were to evangelize, disciple and build the church. If someone got too close to the local people, they surmised, he or she could not be objective in accomplishing the task. Their reasoning seemed feeble.

Chuck believed he was there to serve the people, which certainly included getting to know them, understanding their culture and fitting in. That required time together, not just in business or strategy meetings but in the flow of life and leisure. While the relationships with local people prospered, the opposite was true with his missionary colleagues. He was increasingly left out of events, overlooked in various ways and effectively marginalized. He increasingly thought about quitting before completing the term. Clouds of discouragement settled in, and life held little joy. The fog was dense—the mystery nearly crushing.

At the end of his term of service Chuck returned to the United States, pursued some additional education and became involved in ministry. While the days were bright and exciting, the fog still hung over that earlier period of his life.

Ten years later, Chuck returned to the country and began looking up old acquaintances. One pastor, part of the circle of relationships the missionary had enjoyed, asked him to preach at his church. Visitors are often extended this honor. Early in the service the pastor made some reference to a special person in the congregation who "changed the history of missions in this country." Chuck scanned the 350 or so people but saw no one from his previous years that he recognized who might have earned such recognition. Later, the local pastor repeated the statement as he was introducing Chuck to speak. Puzzlement came over the missionary, thinking he was being confused with someone else. His legacy had been a few relationships and a lot of fog. The pastor continued, "This man invited many of us into his home. Not only that, he brought us through the front door. Then we sat in his living room and ate at his table. No other missionaries did that in those days. Now nearly all the missionaries invite us into their homes through the front door and treat us as honored guests—as equals. In this way, he changed the history of missions in our country." After ten years of fog, it all lifted in less than one minute. The mystery was explained.

God chose to work behind the scenes in a wonderful way that took missionary and national relationships to a new level. God is trustworthy even when we can't see, feel or hear him. He guides us in decisions and promises never to leave us, even when his guidance takes us into the fog, mystery and suffering. He is there in the fog, he is active, and he is fulfilling his glorious purposes. Our role is to trust—even if it takes ten years.

THE BATTLE OF MIND AND EMOTIONS

When walking in a fog the normal clues that orient us are gone. We look for some sign to show us the way, but none appear. Heaven seems silent. We search for meaning in life, but the fog hides it. We plead, "God, why don't you do something?" Our feelings tell us that God must be somewhere else or he doesn't care. The mind, grounded in the Scripture, fires back, "Not true." God has promised to never, not ever, leave us. And so the feelings and the mind thrash about, each submitting evidence for its position.

Sooner or later, often later, the fog slowly lifts. Things begin to make sense. Understanding replaces confusion. Confidence replaces doubt. Belonging replaces a sense of abandonment. Hope returns. God was there all along, working actively, not only on your behalf but in ways that enrich the many other servants he loves. The fog obscures his presence and his purposes, but when it finally clears, we realize that God has kept all his promises to us (see Josh 21:45). And on those occasions when his people go to the grave with pieces of their past still shrouded in fog, he remains the loving, faithful God worthy of their trust even though the fog never lifted. While not desired, walking in mystery shouldn't be feared; God, though not visible or audible, walks by our side, and the walk is always worthwhile for the patient, faithful servant.

Perhaps because Westerners exercise so much control over their lives, they've grown unaccustomed to mystery. Most people in the world don't have the resources to exercise such control over their lives. Take insurance, for example. Those in the West have car, life, home, flood, earthquake, health, credit card and appliances insurance. But just in case, many also buy an umbrella insurance policy to cover what might remain uninsured. People with resources have a multitude of ways of protecting themselves against the unknown, but those without sufficient resources are vulnerable. Paradoxically, people of the Two-Thirds World still seem to enjoy more peace of mind than those of us who exercise more control over our lives. How do they do it? We would do well to learn from them about contentment amidst mystery.

When the fog threatens our judgment, we must cling to unassailable truths, such as:

- God has promised never to leave me. Therefore God is near even though the fog hides his presence and I fear he may have abandoned me.

- God keeps his promises. In spite of my circumstances and past acts, he does not, will not and cannot change his mind about walking with me during the mystery times.

- God works his good purposes not only for me but for all he loves. In life's mysteries he is actively working out his good pleasure for me and for others even though I may never realize it.

- Even if the fog of mystery never lifts in my life, God is worthy of my worship and obedience. He may choose not to explain himself, and I must rest in his wise judgment. Deuteronomy 29:29 states, "The secret things belong to the LORD our God, but the things revealed belong to us and to our children forever, that we may follow all the words of this law."

- My responsibility is to walk humbly and faithfully before my just and loving God and within my community.

MYSTERY'S BIGGEST STRESSOR

I just returned from Southeast Asia, where I spent a couple weeks with missionaries. Most of those I met were experiencing considerable stress. About six couples confessed they had seriously considered going home early during the previous year. The fog was dense and relentless; there was no sign of relief. The stressor? Interpersonal conflict among the missionaries. They couldn't get along with one another, and living in conflict was more than they could bear. While there are cultural stressors from living in a new and very different culture, most missionaries adjust. Living with other missionaries seems to be more difficult. In my extensive travel there have been relatively few situations where interpersonal breakdown has not been the foremost challenge missionaries face. It is the mystery hardest to bear.

Many short-term teams experience this same kind of stress in their brief time together. Yet few help team members prepare for this type of mystery and, consequently, a shadow falls across the experience. While attention is given to health concerns, legal matters, travel documents and ministry activities, little time is given to life together. But we are not only called to serve the nationals but to serve one another. Without unity among the missionaries, servanthood to the local people will be severely hampered.

What causes the interpersonal stress? While there might be a multitude of answers, I will only address a few and trust that the discussion will stimulate further thought and action.

Personality differences. People are different. Some people are extroverts and some are introverts; some are boisterous and others quiet; some aggressive and controlling, others are passive. I am quite aware of the type of person that irritates me. I have had to think about why I react negatively to certain people. Is what they are doing somehow inappropriate or just annoying? Do others seem irritated by that person's behavior? Usually when others don't seem as disturbed as I am, I conclude the problem is mine. Then I try to stay open, accept the person who is different from me (they too bear God's image) and build trust.

I also find that most things that irritate me are not that important— not worth fighting for, not worth losing sleep over, not worth the energy of fretting about. When I exercise this perspective, it really helps to let it go and focus on the many good things that are usually going on around me. The good things are a higher priority and deserve my energy. Satan would try to divide Christians over things of little consequence.

Philosophical differences. Most of us are unaware of how philosophical we are. Two people in Southeast Asia were disputing whether a health ministry should take this shape or another. That was a philosophical difference. Others debate about mission priorities: church planting or evangelism or discipleship or leadership development. How we do church planting or evangelism causes conflict. Another big difference is the lifestyles of missionaries—the standard of living in a given country. What kind of vehicle, house, "toys," salary should they have? Missionaries also differ over local schools, international schools, missionary schools and home schools for their children. In some cases, missionaries question how close they ought to get to the nationals. Should they keep a respectful distance or become "best friends" with the local people?

Generational differences. Differences between generations seem a little sharper in recent history, and more painful. My observations and reading suggest the tension often occurs in worship styles, with most younger missionaries preferring greater physical expression, contemporary music, drums and guitars and a more spontaneous, easy style. The older generation, while growing in their acceptance and even appreciation of this kind of worship, may still prefer the more traditional forms. Difficulty comes when a local church seeks guidance on the style of worship they should pursue.

Another generational difference concerns priorities: should we give primary emphasis to relationship building (younger generation) or evangelism, church planting and discipleship (older generation). The younger generation believes that the task emerges naturally from relationships with the local people whereas the older generation, often with a greater sense of urgency, want to see people saved and the church birthed as soon as possible.

Finally, there are differences on authority, commitment and what it means to be a person of faith. Many of my students who have entered missions took a different route getting there. Whereas the older generation simply followed the directives of superiors to go to a certain place and do a certain ministry, my students are inclined to follow their own instincts. For example, the younger generation will visit three or four countries, get to know the people they might be working with and explore the kinds of ministries that interest them. This is all done prayerfully over several months. Then *they* choose the place and ministry. The older generation sees this as an unnecessary expenditure of money, not trusting the authority of mission leaders and lacking faith in God, who works through the mission leadership. Furthermore, most of my students want to go for one to two years to "see if it fits." Again, this is perceived as lack of commitment and faith by older missionaries. These are all tension points as older and younger missionaries work together. However, these competing values need not cause conflict if we realize these are differences not a violation of absolutes.

The older and younger generations do need each other. The stability, maturity and wisdom of the experienced missionaries often provides the parent-and-grandparent nurture many younger missionaries did not receive in their homes. The younger generation, on the other hand, brings energy, vision and new values that might benefit those who have become stale or set in their ways. There *is* a way to make this work by applying the principles taught earlier in this book: (1) remain open by suspending judgment, (2) accept the others and assume that God's wisdom can effectively come through them, (3) build trust so that we think the best about each other, (4) learn from each other as those who are priests, (5) pursue understanding, because God doesn't do his work only through one generation, one ethnicity, one gender or one nationality, and finally (6) we must serve one another with the same passion we serve the local people.

Proximity differences. By *proximity* I mean both geographic and relational. Missionaries must work closely with each other, and often we are unable to choose who we work with. Sometimes we may also live in the same space, such as a compound or village. This means we must get along with the people God has placed around us. We can't choose new friends or colleagues who fit us better. Thus we must make the relationships work, or we will live in perpetual stress and conflict. Long-term conflict (fog) is not all that rare, but it's terribly debilitating. Perhaps that is why the younger missionaries prefer to tour the mission fields before making a commitment. Many of them have experienced sustained conflict in their homes, including divorced parents, and wish to avoid it on the mission field if possible.

Cultural differences. Simply living as a missionary causes stress, especially in the first year or two. The daily discipline of speaking (or trying to speak) another language, figuring out driving patterns, preparing food, maintaining hygiene, relating to others, dealing with children's adjustments and hundreds of unexpected things taxes one's energies. For the first six weeks of our ministry, my wife and I collapsed into bed at night wondering why we were so tired when we did the same activities back home without feeling like this. While we burned about the same physical energy in the daily routine, we burned considerably more emotional energy. That is, our minds were continually working so hard trying to understand our new surroundings. And burning emotional energy left us even more depleted. At the end of the day we had little reserve left to deal with all of the personal, philosophical, proximity and generational differences.

In addition, we had come from a colder climate (Chicago), and adjusting to the hot, humid and sea-level atmosphere took its own toll.

These and other differences create stress in the early years of missionary service (and sometimes beyond the early years) and cause many to wonder if God is with them, if they missed his call, if there is some severe defect in their spiritual life. Then they begin to wonder whether they made a mistake or if it is time to go home. All of these differences can create a really intense fog that clouds our judgment.

SUMMARY

The servant is often called to walk in mystery, perhaps never more so than in cross-cultural ministry. While it's difficult to implement the servant principles and skills along with everything else, doing so will create a foundation for effective ministry—revealing Christ and his love. Eventually, the fog will lift.

One cross-cultural servant walked in enormous mystery, but he did it with dignity and faithfulness to his God. This young man eventually became servant to nations. Joseph is a model for us not only in handling mystery but in leadership and in handling power. He utilized the servant principles we have discussed and shows us that they work.

THE SERVANT MODEL
Joseph

*"Whosoever wants to be first must be your slave—
just as the Son of man came not to be served, but to serve,
and to give his life as a ransom for many"*

MATTHEW 20:27-28

Joseph is among my favorite characters of the Bible. Loved and accepted by his father, rejected and hated by his own brothers, he experienced the best and worst in life. Mystery stalked his life for years through no fault of his own. Forced to live cross-culturally, he responded nobly. Finally, he found himself in a position of enormous power. When the opportunity came to unleash revenge against his brothers for their betrayal, he was gracious and ultimately forgave and was reconciled to them. He chose the towel of service rather than the robe of power and authority.

Through the fog and the sunshine, one phrase keeps recurring: "The LORD was with Joseph." Joseph honored God and walked with him (Gen 40:8, 41:16, 28, 52). No sin is recorded in Joseph's life. That doesn't mean he did not sin but that his life was characterized by loyalty and service to God. God blessed and prospered Joseph, but did not protect him from mysterious trials of life. Yet, during those mystery phases, Joseph acted no differently than when things were going well: he honored God and walked humbly through each day. Joseph doesn't seem to change whether he is second to the most powerful person in the world or left to rot in a dungeon. Servants are like that—no different whether exalted or abased. When it was all over, God had used Joseph to save two nations.

Joseph's early life was anything but ideal. The first son of Jacob and Rachel, Joseph was the favorite of Jacob's eleven sons, symbolized in part by his richly ornamented robe, which probably signaled favored status (Gen 37:3). Joseph's brothers hated him (Gen 37:4) and made life miserable for him. No evidence exists that Joseph brought any of this on himself; though he did seem naive in the way he shared his dream, which inflamed the jealousy of the brothers and befuddled his father (Gen 37:5-11).

One day, Jacob decided to send Joseph to check on his brothers, who were watching the sheep (Gen 37:12-14). The brothers seized this opportunity to express their spite for Joseph. They threw him in an empty cistern before selling him to some passing Midianite merchants en route to Egypt.

THE INVOLUNTARY MISSIONARY

Joseph, a sheltered teenager, now found himself headed for a life of slavery. He had entered a heavy fog, a mystery so deep and disorienting he might not be blamed for denouncing all he believed about God. How could the God of his father, Jacob, be trustworthy when he allowed such injustice? Joseph's real feelings aren't given, but being human he must have experienced intense inner turmoil and a "dark night of the soul." No evidence exists that he doubted or was angry at God. In fact, he seemed to launch into this new culture with composure and purpose. God saw to it that he was sold to Potiphar, a high official in Pharaoh's court. Egypt was the most powerful nation in the world at that time, and Joseph landed in the middle of the ruling elite. "The LORD was with Joseph" (Gen 39:2).

In Potiphar's household Joseph probably started with menial chores, while learning the language and Egyptian culture. Whatever mental and emotional fog he may have experienced, he did his job well. Even Potiphar noticed that "the LORD was with him and that the LORD gave him success in everything he did." So much so that "Joseph found favor in [Potiphar's] eyes and became his attendant" (Gen 39:3-4). Joseph was promoted to being responsible for all Potiphar owned.

Later, Joseph was unjustly thrown in prison, and the prison warden noted the same thing that Potiphar had (Gen 39:23). Did these men know the Hebrews believed in the Lord God? Or did Joseph tell them about the Lord? Joseph repeatedly insists on crediting God for his abilities (Gen 39:9; 40:8; 41:16). In a situation where Joseph might have been sorely tempted to "puff" himself by taking credit for the remarkable interpretation of dreams, he exhibited the first quality of a servant: humility. This virtue, when prominent in a person's life, always features God as the source of all that is good.

THE JOSEPH MODEL

Openness. Potiphar found Joseph to be such a safe person of integrity that he entrusted him with the oversight of his entire estate. The prison warden found the same quality in Joseph and gave him oversight of all the prisoners. Eventually Pharaoh made Joseph second in command of the entire nation. God's presence with Joseph and Joseph's ability to connect with people in positive ways made him stand out in the eyes of the world. Joseph always welcomed people into his presence and made them feel safe. By embracing Egyptian culture and by embracing those God put around him, Joseph revealed the presence of the Lord and the aroma of heaven in all his conduct. His ability to suspend judgment and remain open allowed God to work through him.

Acceptance. How did Joseph—a young slave in a strange land—communicate acceptance to his owners? He did what any wise person would do: he discovered how they communicated acceptance and practiced it.

But Joseph did more than just adopt the ways of this new culture; he brought a distinctive to it. In particular, Joseph knew how to communicate respect to everyone around him, and they promoted him. Joseph recognized his captors' dignity. He treated them not as enemies or oppressors but as those who bore the image of the Creator—the Creator he wished to serve.

Like Joseph, we need to do what the local people do and fit in as much as possible without violating our faith. Fitting in is not a sign that we have no convictions. Rather, it's a sign of maturity. Most of life is a matter of nonessential differences. Most cultural differences are not worth fighting against. Yes, we must reject those few things that may clearly violate our biblically based conscience. But we need to look for ways to address them without offense. The gospel is offensive, but we don't need to be. When we sensitively do this, we'll find others open and accepting toward us.

It appears Joseph adjusted so well that when his brothers visited Egypt some years later, they saw an Egyptian ruler, not their own brother (Gen 42:8). Because Joseph accepted his new culture, God protected two nations. We never know what God has in mind when he calls us to follow him.

Trust. How do we earn the trust of others? What do others do to earn our trust? What is the role of trust in life's relationships? In marriage? In rearing children? In being an employer or employee? In developing a ministry in another culture? Joseph did it extremely well. He learned the language, excelled in his daily chores, honored people, didn't complain about the bumps in his life, forgave those who mistreated him and in times of mystery persevered with a deep confidence that God would stay near.

Joseph built trust so effectively that each authority (Potiphar, the warden, Pharaoh) turned their world over to Joseph. Joseph built trust by keeping his masters' best interests in mind. He not only extended trust to others but the others returned the trust, giving Joseph a strategic place from which to fulfill God's purposes. The Egyptian leaders did this knowing full well Joseph's faith commitment. It seems Joseph did two things extremely well: he adjusted to the cultural patterns that were simply matters of difference (language, dress, social customs), and he did not compromise biblical principles (honesty, worship of the one true God, avoiding self-serving motives and humbly serving others).

As we build trust with others in a new culture, they will naturally reciprocate by trusting us with important parts of their lives. From that place of deep mutual trust, the purposes of God will emerge. And this can happen without compromising our deepest beliefs.

Learning. How did Joseph keep getting promoted? He gave himself to learning the Egyptian language and adapting to Egyptian culture, and he did it well. Joseph learned the Egyptian culture so well that he managed its affairs, and it prospered wondrously. Yet he remained uncontaminated by corruption, avoided the scheming to get ahead, worked in the best interest of others, was forthright but not forceful about his faith and stayed focused on his God whose purposes were, for much of his life, hidden from him. Centuries before Jesus walked this earth, Joseph understood that "whoever wants to be first must be your slave—just as the Son of man came not to be served, but to serve, and to give his life as a ransom for many" (Mt 20:28).

Understanding. Could Joseph have run a nation without understanding its political, relational, economic and commercial intricacies—its tapestry? Could he have been effective without a willingness to work within the Egyptian cultural patterns? His astounding effectiveness resided in his ability to adjust to the rhythms of Egyptian life without compromising his essence as a God-fearing Hebrew. Understanding takes time, vigilance, a willingness to change in the face of the new and different. Joseph, like many missionaries over the years, so identified with his adopted home that at his death he was embalmed—just like the Egyptians (Gen 50:26).

Serving. Joseph served God humbly and obediently through the good times and bad. In the end he served (saved!) the nation of Egypt and the family of Jacob. A fitting epitaph for Joseph is recorded near the end of his life as his brothers fearfully appear before him. Joseph said to them, "Don't be afraid. Am I in the place of God? You intended to harm me, but God intended it for good to accomplish what is now being done, the saving of many lives" (Gen 50:19-20).

In the end Joseph, a cross-cultural servant, engaged people in positive ways, adjusted to the cultural realities and fulfilled God's purposes without compromising his faith. His work was exceptional, his character proven to be above reproach and his motivation drawn from a kingdom not of this world. In times of intense mystery, he was neither doubtful nor bitter. In fact, it seemed to strengthen his belief that the God of Abraham, Isaac and Jacob was the one true God who would never leave nor forsake him. Then, like any good servant of the Lord, he chose to accept what God gave him, and he prospered despite the circumstances. "The LORD was with him." And he is with us.

CONCLUDING THOUGHTS

Practice openness toward people, accept them as they are and build trust with them. This is the foundation for revealing Christ to others, even when you are in a new culture for only a short time.

Learn from the people. They will feel valued, and your presence will be a positive experience for them. Whatever else you accomplish will be a bonus. Refrain from correcting or judging the local people; instead, ask why? Seek understanding; study the local people and their ways with an open mind. Then you will be liked, and those you've touched will grieve at your departure.

Practice serving others before you enter another culture. Develop these primary building blocks while in your comfort zone, and you will be prepared for applying the same attitudes and skills elsewhere. These same building blocks will help you be successful in other parts of life—marriage, friendships and vocation—wherever God places you. There are no boundaries on the practice of servanthood.

God has a significant role for you in his global mission. But it can be significant only if you are able to follow the servanthood of Jesus, which is difficult in the best of circumstances but especially challenging in places that are foreign to you. Yet God calls all Christians to this life and assures us that we will never be more like Jesus than when we serve.

> You are my servant;
>   I have chosen you and have not rejected you.
> So do not fear, for I am with you;
>   do not be dismayed, for I am your God.
> I will strengthen you and help you;
>   I will uphold you with my righteous right hand. (Is 41:9-10)

Chapter 1: Servanthood: Its Burdens and Challenge

[1]Craig Storti, *Cross-Cultural Dialogues* (Yarmouth, Me.: Intercultural Press, 1994), p. 47.

Chapter 2: Servanthood: Choosing the Towel or the Robe

[1]James C. Edgar, "Dress," in *Wycliffe Bible Dictionary,* ed. Charles F. Pfeiffer, Howard F. Vos and John Rea (Peabody, Mass.: Hendrickson, 1975), p. 481.

[2]B. O. Banwell, "Foot," in *New Bible Dictionary,* ed. J. D. Douglas, 3rd ed. (Downers Grove, Ill.: InterVarsity Press, 1997), p. 380.

Chapter 3: Humility: Posture of the Servant

[1]I revisit this story from an earlier book to make yet another point. The story originally appeared in my *Cross-Cultural Connections* (Downers Grove, Ill.: InterVarsity Press, 2002), p. 14. Ann Templeton Brownlee, I am told, has originated the story of the monkey and the fish. I was unable to locate the source. The version in the text is my own, and the degree this story overlaps with that of Ms. Brownlee is unknown.

[2]See Kenneth Wuest, "Humility," in *Studies in the Vocabulary of the Greek New Testament* (Grand Rapids: Eerdmans, 1945), pp. 100-105.

[3]Ibid., p. 101.

[4]This negative view of humility is based on conversations with believers in former communist countries in Central and Eastern Europe as well as in China.

[5]Philip Yancey, "Humility's Many Faces," *Christianity Today,* December 4, 2000, p. 96.

[6]Ibid.

[7]William Barclay, *The Letters to Philippians, Colossians and Thessalonians* (Edinburgh: Saint Andrew's Press, 1960), p. 40.

[8]Richard G. Capen Jr., *Living the Values That Take You the Distance* (New York: Harper, 1996), p. 80.

9"Willowbank Report: Gospel and Culture," Lausanne Occasional Papers 2 (Lausanne Committee for World Evangelization, 1978), pp. 15-16.

10Millard Erickson, *Christian Theology* (Grand Rapids: Baker, 1998), p. 131.

Chapter 4: Openness: Welcoming Others into Your Presence

1David Schuringa, *Today: The Family Altar, May-June 2002,* June 2, 2002.

2The experience of the European visitors was told to me by Ryan Smith, who took the group to the church on July 12, 2004.

3Miroslav Volf, *Exclusion and Embrace* (Nashville: Abingdon, 1996), p. 29.

4Stephen Rhodes, *Where the Nations Meet* (Downers Grove, Ill.: InterVarsity Press, 1998), p. 134.

5Ibid., p. 135.

6This story was told by a manuscript reviewer in July 2005, who anonymously contributed wonderful insights to the first draft of this book. Printed with the permission of the reviewer.

7I wrote down the results of the study but unfortunately did not record the bibliographical information. However, Malcolm Gladwell, in his book *Blink* (New York: Little, Brown, 2005), records numerous illustrations of quick judgments often at the unconscious or preconscious level. He calls it "thin slicing," meaning that people form judgments with only a fraction of the total information available and virtually no conscious thought. Gladwell offers both the pros and cons of this tendency.

8I addressed negative attribution in my *Cross-Cultural Connections* book. Since it is such a powerful idea and since negative attribution tends to negate or close down our being open to others, it is necessary to revisit it here.

9To read more extensively, see the work of Netherlands university professor Geert Hofstede, *Cultures and Organizations: Software of the Mind* (New York: McGraw-Hill, 1997). One major theme of his book is uncertainty avoidance, which he equates with tolerance for ambiguity. His book is based on extensive research of corporate cultures in fifty countries across three regions of the world. The more recent edition includes some former Soviet Union countries. See also works by Carley Dodd and William Gudykunst cited in the bibliography.

10Steven B. Sample, *The Contrarian's Guide to Leadership* (San Francisco: Jossey-Bass, 2002), p. 7.

11Lesslie Newbigin, cited in Rhodes, *Where the Nations Meet,* p. 58.

Chapter 5: Acceptance: Communicating Respect for Others

1Carley Dodd, *Dynamics of Intercultural Communication,* 2nd ed. (Dubuque, Iowa: Wm. C. Brown, 1987), p. 224.

[2]Dallas Willard, *Renovation of the Heart* (Colorado Springs, Colo.: NavPress, 2002), p. 36.

[3]I encourage you to read pages 91-97 in my book, *Cross-Cultural Connections* (Downers Grove, Ill.: InterVarsity Press, 2002), where I deal with basic concept of acceptance.

[4]Gary Smalley and John Trent, cited in Stephen Rhodes, *Where the Nations Meet* (Downers Grove, Ill.: InterVarsity Press, 1998), p. 42.

[5]Ibid.

[6]Ibid.

[7]Ibid., p. 44.

[8]Darrow Miller, *Servanthood: The Vocation of the Christian, A Monograph* (Scottsdale, Ariz.: Food for the Hungry, 1991), p. 109.

[9]"Why the Holocaust," an interview with Helmut Thielicke, *Christianity Today,* January 27, 1978, p. 8.

[10]Ibid., p. 10.

[11]Ibid., p. 11.

[12]C. S. Lewis, "The Weight of Glory," in *The Essential C. S. Lewis,* ed. Lyle W. Dorsett (New York: Collier, 1988), p. 369.

[13]See T. F. Pettigrew, "Cognitive Styles and Social Behavior," in *Review of Personality and Social Psychology,* ed. L. Wheeler (Beverly Hills, Calif.: Sage, 1982), 3:200. If you want to take a short quiz to help you determine your own category width, one can be found in William Gudykunst, *Bridging Differences,* 4th ed. (Thousand Oaks, Calif.: Sage, 2004), p. 175; Robert Detwiler, "Culture, Category Width and Attributions," *Journal of Cross-Cultural Psychology* 11 (1978); and Robert Detwiler "Intercultural Interaction and the Categorization Process," *International Journal of Intercultural Relations* 4 (1980).

[14]Pettigrew, "Cognitive Styles," p. 207; see also Gudykunst, *Bridging Differences,* pp. 17-18, 173-75.

[15]Robert Detwiler, "On Inferring the Intentions of a Person from Another Culture," *Journal of Personality* 43 (1975): 600.

[16]Carley H. Dodd, *Dynamics of Intercultural Communication,* 5th ed. (New York: McGraw-Hill, 1998), p. 275.

[17]Ibid., p. 179.

[18]E. Zerubavel, *The Fine Line* (New York: Free Press, 1991), p. 34.

[19]Gudykunst, *Bridging Differences,* p. 162.

[20]See "Worship Expressions: From High to Low," in my *Cross-Cultural Connections,* pp. 182-90.

[21]David W. Johnson, *Reaching Out* (Englewood Cliffs, N.J.: Prentice-Hall, 1972), pp. 129-31.

[22]Sherwood G. Lingenfelter and Marvin K. Mayers, *Ministering Cross-Culturally,* 2nd ed. (Grand Rapids: Baker, 2003), pp. 66-67.

Chapter 6: Trust: Building Confidence in Relationships

[1]Ann T. Fraker and Larry C. Spears, eds. *Seeker and Servant: Reflections on Religious Leadership* (San Francisco: Jossey-Bass, 2001), p. 89.

[2]This illustration is also used in my book *Cross-Cultural Connections* (Downers Grove, Ill.: InterVarsity Press, 2002), pp. 36-37.

[3]I've selected a few wonderful verses from the book of Psalms that speak of God's trustworthiness: Ps 36:5; 89:1, 24; 92:2; 119:86, 90, 138. Also from Psalms, verses that call for our trust in God: Ps 40:4; 73:28.

[4]Richard G. Capen Jr., *Living the Values That Take You the Distance* (New York: Harper, 1996), pp. 70, 75.

[5]See *Cross-Cultural Conflict,* where I deal with handling conflict at length.

[6]Most mediators in this context would be men.

Chapter 7: Learning: Seeking Information That Changes You

[1]I rehearse this story because I still see the same lingering attitudes, especially among my (older) generation. I have also noticed it in missionaries who have gone out from the Two-Thirds World countries (e.g., India, Cambodia, Bolivia, Zambia). Thus I am inclined to think it is a human tendency that still needs to be addressed.

[2]I am using *education* here in the most popular sense. I often differentiate education from schooling for the sake of precision. More schooling does not necessarily mean being better educated. Many highly schooled people are not, in my opinion, well educated. Educated people are marked by knowledge, to be sure. But beyond that, they are marked by humility, which keeps them open to learning from others throughout their life. They are also marked by being good practitioners of what they know. Many argue that knowing without doing is not to know. Thus we all struggle with the problem of the Pharisees who knew truth but did not practice it (Mt 23).

[3]I am aware that we can learn about people while in the culture itself. This can be done by reading, taking a class, observing art or using other means of gathering information. While this can be helpful and legitimate, it doesn't bring us into direct contact with the people; there are limitations and even dangers.

[4]Daniel J. Kealey, "The Challenge of International Personnel Selection," *Handbook of Intercultural Training,* ed. D. Bhagat Landis and R. S. Bhagat Landis (Thousand Oaks, Calif.: Sage, 1996), pp. 84-89. Kealey has dropped *realistic* in his recent research because it has been too elusive to measure accurately. I, however, continue to use it as a descriptor alerting us to the fact that life has "ups and downs" everywhere. As

such, we are more likely to avoid the extremes of overly positive or overly negative about living in another culture.

[5]Reuel L. Howe, *The Miracle of Dialogue* (Minneapolis: Seabury, 1963), pp. 36, 37.

[6]I am writing from my American perspective; I know the majority of the missionary force is now from the Two-Thirds World, who also experience these same realities. However, they need to speak for themselves on these issues. In so doing, we will learn what is universal to humankind in crossing cultures and what may be specific to cultures.

Chapter 8: Learning Biblical Foundations for Change

[1]Paul Enns, *The Moody Handbook of Theology* (Chicago: Moody Press, 1989), p. 332; and Millard J. Erickson, *Christian Theology,* 2nd ed. (Grand Rapids: Baker, 1998), p. 321.

[2]Louis Berkhof, *Systematic Theology,* 4th ed. (Grand Rapids: Eerdmans, 1941), p. 436.

[3]Romans 1:20 goes on to say that he has revealed his "eternal power and divine nature" and these "have been clearly seen, being understood from what has been made, so that men are without excuse." The text clearly states that people without Christ have no excuse for rejecting him. Thus the people of God, those who are followers of Christ, must share the gospel of God's saving grace through his Son Jesus so that people may repent and become worshipers of the one true God. Common grace, recognizing God's existence and kindness in the world around us, is intended to lead people to receive his special grace of salvation through the convicting work of the Holy Spirit and turning to Christ, the solution to our sin problem (Jn 16:8-11).

[4]If you have little or no awareness of the central value that shame, losing face and honor play in many cultures of the world, you may want to read on the topic lest you cause serious conflict and violate relationships without even knowing it. A knowledge of shame-based cultures will guide your conversations, aid in handling conflict, protect you in handling cultural differences and make you much more effective in building strong relationships and accomplishing other goals. You may wish to start with my book *Cross-Cultural Conflict* (Downers Grove, Ill.: InterVarsity Press, 2002).

[5]See Acts 4:32; 15:22; Rom 12; 1 Cor 12; see also Millard Erickson, *Christian Theology,* 2nd ed. (Grand Rapids: Baker, 1998), pp. 1096-97; "Priesthood" and "Priests and Levites" in *Baker Encyclopedia of the Bible,* ed. Walter Elwell, (Grand Rapids: Baker, 1988), 2:1754-64.

[6]Paul Goring, "What Does It Take to Communicate?" *Decision,* January 1991, pp. 27-28.

[7]I found this William Stringfellow quote in *Friend's Journal*. I have no further information. It can also be found on the International Listening Association's website at <www.listen.org/quotations/morequotes.html>.

[8]Carl Rogers, quoted in David W. Johnson, *Reaching Out* (Englewood Cliffs, N.J.: Prentice-Hall, 1970), pp. 129-31.

[9]Gladis DePree, *The Spring Wind* (New York: Harper & Row, 1970), p. 100.

Chapter 9: Understanding: Seeing Through the Other's Eyes

[1]Sherwood G. Lingenfelter and Marvin K. Mayers, *Ministering Cross-Culturally*, 2nd ed. (Grand Rapids: Baker, 2003), p. 23.

[2]William Gudykunst and Young Yun Kim, *Communicating with Strangers* (New York: McGraw-Hill, 1992), p. 15.

[3]Cornelius Osgood, *The Chinese: A Study of a Hong Kong Community* (Tucson: University of Arizona Press, 1975), p. 15.

[4]David Hesselgrave, *Communicating Christ Cross-Culturally* (Grand Rapids: Zondervan, 1978), p. 69.

[5]Robert Selman calls this perspective-taking, but sometimes it is called perspectivism (*The Promotion of Social Awareness* [New York: Russell Sage Foundation, 2003]). A kindred idea is multicentrism, which is the opposite of egocentrism. Jack Mezirow's "perspective transformation" relies, to some degree, on the ability to take another's perspective in order to transform one's own perspective (*Transformational Dimensions of Adult Learning* [San Francisco: Jossey-Bass, 1991]).

[6]Researchers have identified many more barriers to cross-cultural understanding.

[7]Carley Dodd, *Dynamics of Intercultural Communication*, 5th ed.(Boston: McGraw-Hill, 1998), p. 276.

[8]W. G. Sumner, *Folkways: A Study of the Sociological Importance of Usages, Manners, Customs, Mores and Morals* (Boston: Ginn, 1941), p. 13

[9]Gladis Depree, *The Spring Wind* (New York: Harper & Row, 1970), p. 5.

[10]Anthropologists call the insiders' perspective the *emic* perspective; the *etic* perspective is seeing as the outsider sees.

[11]For more information on empathy, see William B. Gudykunst, *Bridging Differences*, 4th ed. (Thousand Oaks, Calif.: Sage, 2004), pp. 260-64. Also see Carley Dodd, *Dynamics of Intercultural Communication*, 5th ed. (New York: McGraw-Hill, 1998), pp. 178, 193, 202-4.

[12]Dodd, *Dynamics of Intercultural Communication*, p. 87.

[13]Every culture has ways that the patron-client unwritten contract can be broken.

[14]See chap. 15 on individualism and collectivism in my *Cross-Culture Connections* (Downers Grove, Ill.: InterVarsity Press, 2002).

[15]Jason Saunders, a paper presented for Educational Ministries 643, Wheaton College, Wheaton, Illinois, November 1997.

[16]Paulo Freire, *Education for Critical Consciousness* (New York: Continuum, 1973), p. 38. Having the posture Freire describes results in what Hiebert calls "uncritical contextualization"—the idea that we can dictate the gospel to another culture without any attempt to know and understand that culture. Historically this was called "colonialism" or "paternalism," both considered oppressive and un-Christian. See Paul G. Hiebert, *Anthropological Insights for Missionaries* (Grand Rapids: Baker, 1985), pp. 185-91.

Chapter 10: Serving: Becoming Like Christ to Others

[1]Ted Engstrom, "Look for the Unlikely," in *International Bible Society,* December-January 1989-1990, pp. 3-4, cited in Ted W. Engstrom and Robert C. Larson, *The Fine Art of Friendship* (Nashville: Thomas Nelson, 1985).

[2]The story of the Filipina woman was related by a young Youth With A Mission staff woman in Kailua-Kona, Hawaii, during my lecture series "Culture, Values and Education," at the University of the Nations, December 16, 2002.

[3]The story of the young Asian resting her chin on the shoulder of a stranger was related by a young Youth With A Mission staff woman in Kailua-Kona, Hawaii, during my lecture series "Culture, Values and Education," at the University of the Nations, December 16, 2002.

[4]Jim Unger, "Herman"; the only date given is June 3.

Chapter 11: The Servant and Leadership

[1]Joe Stowell, *Proclaim,* WMBI, December 4, 2004.

[2]In this book I have discussed pride, which I see as the subtle and ever-present enemy of humility, but the Bible uses the strongest terms to prompt vigilance in guarding against it.

[3]Lawrence Richards, *Theology of Christian Education* (Grand Rapids: Zondervan, 1980), p. 133.

[4]Francis Schaeffer, *No Little People, No Little Places* (Downers Grove, Ill.: InterVarsity Press, 1974), p. 25.

[5]I am aware of several situations where good local leadership in the church has been siphoned off for more lucrative positions with Christian NGOs (nongovernment organizations), thus depriving the church of local talent. But I am also aware of situations where missionaries find it difficult to trust local leaders or to step aside to let local leaders exercise their gifts. Complicating factors abound, so generalizations are dangerous.

Chapter 12: The Servant and Power

[1]Abraham Zaleznik, "Managers and Leaders," in *Harvard Business Review on Leadership,* ed. Henry Mintzberg, John P. Kotter and Abraham Zaleznik (Boston: Harvard Business School Press, 1998), p. 63.

[2]Maxie Dunnam, *The Workbook on Spiritual Disciplines* (Nashville: Upper Room, 1984), p. 101.

[3]C. Gene Wilkes, *Discovering the Secrets of Servant Leadership from the Life of Christ* (Wheaton, Ill.: Tyndale House, 1998), p. 102.

[4]I say "together" because in Mt 20:20 it indicates the mother did the talking and in Mk 10:35-39 it indicates that James and John did the talking. What this tells me is that the mother and her two sons were of one accord.

Chapter 13: The Servant and Mystery

[1]See Stephen Motyer, "Mystery," in *Evangelical Dictionary of Theology,* ed. Walter Elwell (Grand Rapids: Baker, 1984), p. 742.

BIBLIOGRAPHY

Athen, Gary. *American Ways*. Yarmouth, Me.: Intercultural Press, 1988.

Banwell, B. O., "Foot." In *New Bible Dictionary*, edited by J. D. Douglas, 3rd ed. Downers Grove, Ill.: InterVarsity Press, 1997.

Barclay, William. *The Letters to Philippians, Colossians and Thessalonians*. Edinburgh: Saint Andrew Press, 1959.

Bennis, Warren. *Why Leaders Can't Lead*. San Francisco: Jossey-Bass, 1990.

Berkhof, Louis. *Systematic Theology*. 4th ed. Grand Rapids: Eerdmans, 1941.

Black, J. S., and H. B. Gregersen. "Antecedents to Cross-Cultural Adjustment for Expatriates in Pacific Rim Assignments." *Human Relations* 44 (1991).

Borden, George A. *Cultural Orientation*. Englewood Cliffs, N.J.: Prentice-Hall, 1991.

Brueggemann, Walter. *The Creative Word*. Philadelphia: Fortress, 1982.

Burns, J. Patout, ed. *Theological Anthropology*. Philadelphia: Fortress, 1981.

Capen, Richard G., Jr. *Living the Values That Take You the Distance*. New York: Harper, 1996.

Condon, John C. *With Respect to the Japanese*, edited by George C. Renwick. Interact. Yarmouth, Me.: Intercultural Press, 1984.

Covey, Stephen R. *Principle-Centered Leadership*. New York: Simon & Schuster, 1991.

DePree, Gladis *The Spring Wind*. New York: Harper & Row. 1970.

Dinges, N. G., and K. D. Baldwin. "Intercultural Competence: A Research Perspective." In *Handbook of Intercultural Training*, edited by D. Bhagat Landis and R. S. Bhagat Landis. Thousand Oaks, Calif.: Sage, 1996.

Dodd, Carley H. *Dynamics of Intercultural Communication*. 5th ed. New York: McGraw-Hill, 1998.

Dorsett, Lyle W., ed. *The Essential C. S. Lewis*. New York: Macmillan, 1988.

Dunnam, Maxie. *The Workbook on Spiritual Disciplines*. Nashville: The Upper Room, 1984.

Elmer, Duane H. *Cross-Cultural Conflict: Building Relationships for Effective Ministry*. Downers Grove, Ill.: InterVarsity Press, 1993.

———. *Cross-Cultural Connections: Stepping Out and Fitting In Around the World*. Downers Grove, Ill.: InterVarsity Press, 2002.

Elmer, Duane H., and Lois McKinney, eds. *With an Eye on the Future: Development and Mission in the 21st Century*. Monrovia, Calif.: MARC, 1996.

Edgar, James C. "Dress." In *Wycliffe Bible Dictionary*. Edited by Charles F. Pfeiffer, Howard F. Vos and John Rea. Peabody, Mass: Hendrickson, 1975.

Engstrom, Ted. "Look for the Unlikely." In *International Bible Society*, December-January 1989-1990.

Enns, Paul. *The Moody Handbook of Theology*. Chicago: Moody Press, 1989.

Erickson, Millard J. *Christian Theology*. 2nd ed. Grand Rapids: Baker, 1998.

Ferris, Robert F. "Servanthood, His and Ours." Lectures given at the Conservative Baptist Mission Annual Conference, Tagaytay City, Philippines, 1984.

Fitzsimmonds, F. S. "Humility." In *New Bible Dictionary*, edited by J. D. Douglas. Grand Rapids: Eerdmans, 1962.

Foster, Richard, *Celebration of Discipline*. New York: Harper Collins, 1988

Fox, Christine. "The Authenticity of Intercultural Communication." *International Journal of Intercultural Relations* 21, no. 1 (1997).

Fraker, Ann T., and Larry C. Spears, eds. *Seeker and Servant: Reflections on Religious Leadership*. San Francisco: Jossey-Bass, 1996.

Freire, Paulo. *Education for Critical Consciousness*. New York: Continuum, 1973.

Goring, Paul. "What Does It Take to Communicate?" *Decision*, January 1991.

Gudykunst, William B. *Bridging Differences*. 4th ed. Thousand Oaks, Calif.: Sage, 2004.

Gudykunst, William B., and Stella Ting-Toomey. *Culture and Interpersonal Communication*. Thousand Oaks, Calif.: Sage, 1988.

Gudykunst, William B., and Young Yun Kim. *Communicating with Strangers*. Menlo Park, Calif.: Addison-Wesley, 1984.

———. *Communicating with Strangers*. 2nd ed. New York: McGraw-Hill, 1992.

———. *Readings on Communicating with Strangers*. New York: McGraw-Hill, 1992.

Gudykunst, William B., Lea P. Stewart and Stella Ting-Toomey, eds. *Communication, Culture, and Organizational Processes*. International and Intercultural Communication Annual 29. Thousand Oaks, Calif.: Sage, 1985.

Harris, John. *Facilitating Others: A Christian View of Leadership*. Alabaster, Ala.: Smokey Road, 2003.

Hawes, Frank, and Daniel J. Kealey. "An Empirical Study of Canadian Technical Assistance: Adaptation and Effectiveness on Overseas Assignments." *International Journal of Intercultural Relations*, no. 4 (1981).

Hiebert, Paul G. *Anthropological Insights for Missionaries*. Grand Rapids: Baker, 1985.

————. *Missiological Implications of Epistemological Shifts: Affirming Truth in a Modern/Postmodern World*. Harrisburg, Penn.: Trinity Press International, 1999.

Hoekema, Anthony A. *Created in God's Image*. Grand Rapids: Eerdmans, 1986.

Hopler, Tom, and Marcia Hopler. *Reaching the World Next Door.* Downers Grove, Ill.: InterVarsity Press, 1993.

Howard, C. "Profile of the 21st Century Expatriate Manager." *Human Relations* (1992).

Howe, Reuel L. *The Miracle of Dialogue*. Minneapolis: Seabury, 1963.

Huxley, Aldous. *Along the Road*. Freeport, N.Y.: Books for Libraries Press, 1972.

Johnson, David W. *Reaching Out*. Englewood Cliffs, N.J.: Prentice Hall, 1972.

Kealey, Daniel J. "The Challenge of International Personnel Selection." In *Handbook of Intercultural Training*, edited by D. Bhagat Landis and R. S. Bhagat Landis. Thousand Oaks, Calif.: Sage, 1996.

————. *Cross-Cultural Effectiveness: A Study of Canadian Technical Advisors Overseas*. Hull, Quebec: Canadian International Development Agency, 1990.

Kohls, L. Robert. *Developing Intercultural Awareness*. Washington, D.C.: SIETAR, 1981.

————. *Survival Kit for Overseas Living*. 2nd ed. Yarmouth, Me.: Intercultural Press, 1984.

Kohls, L. Robert, and John M. Knight. *Developing Intercultural Awareness*. 2nd ed. Yarrnouth, Me.: Intercultural Press, 1994.

Lewis, C. S. *The Weight of Glory and Other Sermons*. New York: Macmillan, 1949.

Lingenfelter, Sherwood G., and Marvin K. Mayers. *Ministering Cross-Cul-*

turally. 2nd ed. Grand Rapids: Baker, 2003.

Mezirow, Jack. *Transformative Dimensions of Adult Learning.* San Francisco: Jossey-Bass, 1991.

Miller, Darrow L. *Servanthood: The Vocation of the Christian, A Monograph.* Scottsdale, Ariz.: Food for the Hungry, 1991.

Motyer, Stephen. "Mystery." In *Evangelical Dictionary of Theology,* edited by Walter Elwell. Grand Rapids: Baker, 1984.

Osgood, Cornelius. *The Chinese: A Study of a Hong Kong Community.* Tucson: University of Arizona Press, 1975.

"A Profile of the Interculturally Effective Person." Centre for Intercultural Learning (2000).

Richards, Lawrence. *Theology of Christian Education.* Grand Rapids: Zondervan, 1980.

Rhodes, Stephen A. *Where the Nations Meet: The Church in a Multicultural World.* Downers Grove, Ill.: InterVarsity Press, 1998.

Sample, Steven B. *The Contrarian's Guide to Leadership.* San Francisco: Jossey-Bass, 2002.

Schaeffer, Francis. *No Little People, No Little Places.* Downers Grove, Ill.: InterVarsity Press, 1974.

Selman, Robert. *The Promotion of Social Awareness.* New York: Russell Sage Foundation, 2003.

Sproul, R. C. *In Search of Dignity.* Ventura, Calif.: Regal Books, 1983.

Stewart, Edward C., and Milton Bennett. *American Cultural Patterns.* Rev. ed. Yarmouth, Me.: Intercultural Press, 1991.

Storti, Craig. *Cross-Cultural Dialogues.* Yarmouth, Me.: Intercultural Press, 1994.

Stowell, Joseph. *Proclaim,* WMBI, December 4, 2004.

Sumner, W. G. *Folkways: A Study of the Sociological Importance of Usages, Manners, Customs, Mores and Morals.* Boston: Ginn, 1941.

VanGemeren, Willem A. "Righteousness." In *Baker Encyclopedia of the Bible,* edited by Walter A. Elwell. Vol. 2. Grand Rapids: Baker, 1988.

Volf, Miroslav. *Exclusion and Embrace*. Nashville: Abingdon, 1996.

———. *Living Overseas*. New York: Free Press, 1984.

"Willowbank Report: Gospel and Culture." Lausanne Occasional Papers 2. Lausanne Committee for World Evangelization, 1978.

Wuest, Kenneth S. *Studies in the Vocabulary of the Greek New Testament*. Grand Rapids: Eerdmans, 1945.

Wenzhong, Hu, and Cornelius L. Grove. *Encountering the Chinese*. Yarmouth, Me.: Intercultural Press, 1991.

Wilkes, C. Gene. *Jesus on Leadership: Discovering the Secrets of Servant Leadership from the Life of Christ*. Wheaton, Ill.: Tyndale House, 1998.

Yancey, Philip. "Humility's Many Faces." *Christianity Today*, December 4, 2000.

Zaleznik, Abraham. "Managers and Leaders." In *Harvard Business Review on Leadership*, edited by Henry Mintzberg, John P. Kotter and Abraham Zaleznik. Boston: Harvard Business School Press, 1998.

Zerubavel, E. *The Fine Line*. New York: Free Press, 1991.